Katie's Surprise

JB Price's Novel Novels
More Than Stories

June (JB) Price
Author and Storyteller

order @ local bookstore
jbpricesnovelnovels.com
amazon.com

Callie's Treasures
Jake & Josie's Discovery
Katie's Surprise
Kyle's Secret Challenge

Katie's Surprise

TREASURES HIDDEN IN THE DARKNESS

JB PRICE

WESTBOW
PRESS®
A DIVISION OF THOMAS NELSON
& ZONDERVAN

WestBow Press books may be ordered through booksellers or by contacting:

WestBow Press
A Division of Thomas Nelson & Zondervan
1663 Liberty Drive
Bloomington, IN 47403
www.westbowpress.com
1 (866) 928-1240

Scripture quotations taken from the Holy Bible, New Living Translation, Copyright © 1996, 2004. Used by permission of Tyndale House Publishers, Inc., Wheaton, Illinois 60189. All rights reserved.

ISBN: 978-1-5127-2109-6 (sc)
ISBN: 978-1-5127-2110-2 (hc)
ISBN: 978-1-5127-2108-9 (e)

Library of Congress Control Number: 2015919464

Print information available on the last page.

WestBow Press rev. date: 12/18/2015

Other Books by JB Price

Callie's Treasures
Jake and Josie's Discovery

DANIEL 2:22 (NLT)
He reveals deep and mysterious things and knows what lies
hidden in the darkness, though he is surrounded by light.

PSALM 139:12 (NLT)
But even in darkness, I cannot hide from you. To you the night
shines as bright as the day. Darkness and light are the same to you.

ISAIAH 45: 3 (NLT)
And I will give you treasures hidden in the darkness … secret
riches. I will do this so you may know that I am the Lord.

Dedication

To my non-white family and friends

Through you, I have tasted some of the dregs of racial prejudice while you've had to drink the full measure. You are some of God's treasures hidden in the darkness … His secret riches. I love your beautiful outsides and your matching insides. Thank you for including me in your lives.

A beautiful black lady, who is also one of my best friends, wrote the following thoughts about this story.

> *Katie's Surprise* is one of the best examples of forgiveness and love in the wake of racism I have ever encountered. The story gave me insight into the engrained prejudice some white people uphold as normal and acceptable.
>
> Being black, I've experienced the anger, confusion and tears that come from being a target of racism. By the end of this story, I found those latent by-products giving way to understanding, forgiveness and most importantly, love. I closed the book with hope that there is a way to combat the hatred and racism among us. Experiencing God's love for ourselves enables us to see the beauty of our differences.
>
> I believe Katie's story will give insight to all races into what divides us, and what it will take to bridge the gulf between us … God's vision and heart for all peoples.
>
> Linda Reese Sykes

One

Unless Katie Williams was trapped in the middle of one of her reoccurring dreams, she was now an orphan. She sat on the side of her bed—numb—waiting for tears of sadness and loss, but her sockets were as dry as her parched throat and her heart was as cold as the floor beneath her feet. Guilt and bitterness wasted no time joining her.

After watching five minutes of her own life tick away, she faced the fact her mom's earthly timepiece had stopped. Now what? Her dad had died last year. She had shed no tears for Father Edgar then, and she couldn't generate any for Mother Martha today.

Aunt Bea would attribute that to her anger and bitterness. Could be. She wasn't wise about things like that … thanks in part to her folks. They abandoned their nurturing responsibilities years ago.

Her four-year-old son, JD, was the reason. Their parting words still haunted her at times. "Have an abortion or surrender custody, and you can come back home." The life of her child for their approval and acceptance? Never!

Until this moment, she had no idea how prophetic her last words had been. She shuttered as a faint tinge of regret flittered across the landscape of her mind. What was it Poe's raven kept repeating? *Nevermore.* Exactly. And that's the end of that.

She flipped a switch in her brain and began mapping the course of her day. Contact Aunt Bea. As she dialed, she knew the predictable woman would answer on the third ring ... if she was home.

"Hello, Bertha Evans speaking."

"Did my early morning phone call wake you, Aunt Bea?"

Katie heard Bertha chuckle. "Yeah, I'm surprised a few dead people didn't come knocking on your door."

"I innocently picked up that five-alarm monster at Goodwill yesterday. Now we know why its previous owner so graciously donated it."

"Well, it should have come with a warning. *Not meant for apartment dwellers ... or those living near cemeteries.*"

"Hopefully it has a volume control. By the way the caller was Aunt Edith."

"Edith? What in the world did she want?"

Katie didn't answer immediately. Guilt over her lack of tears and numbness regarding his mom's demise were hammering away at her semi-seared conscience.

"What's going on, Child?"

After relating Edith's message, Katie added, "Guess the trip of my nightmares is calling my name."

"Sorry to hear about your mom. Poor soul. She died without realizing the treasures she had in Roanoke. Never met anybody so worried about what folks think, but then her loss has been my gain."

Two fists knotted as familiar bitterness mushroomed inside Katie. "We both know Mama would rather be dead than admit she had a wayward daughter and an illegitimate grandson. Can't figure out why she'd want me to attend her funeral."

"Youngin, you've hung onto that bitterness and anger long enough. Would be a good thing to bury all that stinking garbage with your mama."

"I don't think they could dig a hole big enough, Aunt Bea." She softened when she heard the sigh on the other end of the line. "Guess you'd better keep me at the top of your prayer list a while longer."

"Honey, I've worn out two sets of knee pads since you moved next door. When are you leaving?"

"If I leave by noon, I should make it by dark. I need to let Kyle know."

"Don't worry about things here." There was a pause. "Barring the reason for the trip, Katie, I'm glad you have to go. You can't ignore the wounds of your past forever."

"Aunt Bea, I love you, but I wish you'd spare me your well-meaning tidbits of wisdom."

Katie heard her familiar groan of exasperation. "Honey, take it from someone who learned from experiences. Heeding wisdom means less time in the School of Hard Knocks."

"Are you kidding me? And give up my shot at valedictorian?"

"You're not as callous as you want folks to think, Katie Williams."

"As long as you don't put an ad in the *Roanoke Times*, my secret is safe, Aunt Bea."

"Get on with you now. Call me when you get there so I can rest easy tonight."

"Yes, Ma'am."

Katie disconnected that call and dialed the only other person on her phone list. She met Kyle while assigned to the Butler Architectural and Design Enterprises as an apprentice her last year at Virginia Tech School of Design.

Thank goodness, those days were over. Katie had been working full-time for Butler Enterprises since her graduation. She planned to move out of this cracker box in a couple of months.

After hearing her news, Kyle offered to go with her. "There's no need for that." Massaging her tense neck muscles kept her from biting her nails.

"When are you leaving?" he asked.

"Hopefully before noon."

"I have a few loose ends to tie up here. Don't go before I get there."

The blessing named Kyle had recently become a problem. He had expressed an interest in more than friendship. In spite of the fact that he was everything a girl could ask for, he set off no fireworks or disturbed any butterflies. He was a trusted friend whom her son adored.

"You're needed at work, Kyle."

"Katie, you are the most important person in my life. In fact, I'm ready to take on the world for you and JD … if you'll let me."

Her body tensed and her tone sharpened. "*My* world will chew you up and spit you out, Kyle. You wouldn't survive."

A confident, yet compassionate voice replied. "You underestimate me, Katie. I could not only survive it, I could make life easier for both of you … if you'll quit being so mule-headed and independent."

His gentleness didn't temper his determination, which was as big as he was … and that was considerable. "Me?" Katie replied. "I don't know much about your family tree, Sir, but I think you got double dipped in the *stubborn* gene pool."

Deep male laughter filled the airwaves. "Then we are a matched pair. I'll be there soon."

She walked into the small bathroom filled with evidence of her son. "Ahoy, Mate! How many pirates have you captured this morning?"

"Today I'm an explorer. Aunt Bea showed me a ball of the whole world yesterday. I'm on one of those big oceans."

Katie could identify with his half dozen, rudderless ships bouncing around aimlessly in the water.

"When I grow up I want to sail around the world, Mama." He started lining his toys up on the side of the tub and released the stopper.

"The world, huh?" She sat on the commode, quickly grabbed a rag and washed the places he likely missed with all his explorations. "How would you like to start today?"

His eyes widened and his feet began catching air and dividing water. As the tidal wave splashed over her and the floor, she groaned. "Maybe I should have saved that surprise until you were out of the ocean."

"Sorry, Mama. I got excited. We never go anywhere."

She encircled his body with a towel. "How would you like to see where I grew up?" His gorgeous green eyes lit up a face with miniature features so like his father's that memories sprang to life.

"Will I get to meet my grandmother … and my daddy?"

How do you explain death … and a dad's absence … to a four-year-old? "JD, your grandmother died, and I don't know if your dad still lives in Asheville."

Sadness clouded his face. "Then why are we going?"

She finger-combed his black, loose curls. "Because it's the right thing to do."

Katie carried the young explorer into the bedroom they had shared the past four years and laid out his clothes. "You get dressed and I'll pack. Put the toys you want to take in the plastic tub."

After locating the Asheville phone directory she had stuffed in her luggage the night they whisked her away, she dialed the Turner Funeral Home. Would Isaac remember her? What had folks heard about her sudden departure? Her heart rate increased when he answered.

"Isaac, this is Katie Williams. Is it true Mom wanted me at her funeral?"

"Yes, Ma'am. Wish the circumstances were different, but it'll be good to see you."

His kind greeting surprised Katie to the point that she struggled to respond.

"No need to fret over arrangements. Martha took care of everything … including the bill. All you have to do is show up."

There was such a logjam in her head that words couldn't reach her mouth. Bless Isaac. He continued as though they were having a two-way conversation.

"Look, Katie, I know your folks didn't do right by you when they were living, but your mom hoped to make up for that in a small way in her dying."

Those words blew the blockade apart. Her nostrils flared and her spine stiffened. "It's a little late, don't you think, Isaac?"

A soft voice answered, "For them, yes. For you, no."

As they hung up, Isaac's words ricocheted off the hardened places in her heart. A lone tear escaped. *Exactly how did you plan to do that, Mama?*

Outside, earth-rattling thunder and jagged bolts of lightning announced the moisture-laden clouds would soon be drenching the historic city nestled in the lower corner of the Shenandoah Valley. Five years in Roanoke had not changed her mind about the town nestled between the Blue Ridge and Appalachian Mountains. Asheville was still her favorite place on the planet. Those thoughts were rummaging through the closets of her past, when she heard a knock at the door. "JD, please let Kyle in."

As soon as the latch released, JD opened the door and leaped into wet arms. "Hold off a minute, Buddy." After hanging his drenched raincoat on the sturdy, Goodwill coat tree, Kyle reached for the curly-headed lad. After exchanging affectionate embraces, he set JD back on his feet. "Let's help your mama."

The lad tugged on Kyle's shirt. "Will you come with us? Grandmother died and Mama doesn't know where my daddy is."

The man stilled for a second before responding. "How would you like for *me* to be your daddy?"

The kid's smile would have shamed the sun had it been shining. "You? Oh, boy. Can you?"

Kyle's gaze shifted to Katie who had heard the exchange. "If your mama agrees."

Her efforts to prepare for this moment proved useless. "This is not the time or place for this discussion, Kyle. JD and I need to get on the road."

"For your information your son has invited me to come along, and I've accepted. And before you go stubborn on me, that is why I'm here. I don't trust that contraption you call *a car*."

"Kyle, you can't leave work …"

His right pointer turned into an upright pendulum as it often did when he was arguing a point. "No protests allowed. I'll take care of the luggage." Depositing JD on the floor and slipping on his raincoat, the big man gathered all four bags under his arms and in his hands and dashed into the storm. The toy tub ended up on the back seat next to JD's car seat. When all were ready, Kyle opened his raincoat. "Come here, Buddy."

Wrapped in the warmth and security of his hero's rain apparel, JD asked, "Is it okay if I call you *Daddy* now?"

As water dripped off his rain slicker, Kyle glanced between the boy and Katie. A lone tear trailed down her cheek. "Katie, you need a husband and this boy wants a daddy. I am applying for both positions. Marry me."

JD wiggled out of Kyle's strong arms and wrapped his small ones around Katie's legs. "Say *yes*, Mama, *please* say *yes*."

Two sets of eyes were pleading and her will crumbled. When she nodded, Kyle removed a small box from his inner pocket and slipped a ring on her finger.

Katie stared at the extravagant proof that she had agreed. "Kyle, I'm a simple girl."

Shucking the still dripping garment, he pulled her into an intimate embrace. "What's the point of having money if you can't spend it on folks you love?"

The kiss left no doubt their relationship had moved up a notch. She was grateful JD was present. The twenty-six-year-old bachelor tucked her son inside his raincoat and headed out the door. "Lock up and let's get on the road."

Two

Every beautiful mile of I-81 made Katie realize how wise Kyle's decision to accompany them was. Besides the inclement weather and a talkative son, a tape of memories of her exile trip was stuck on replay.

Kyle reached for the hand displaying his ring. "Honey, you aren't being rejected or discarded this trip. You are loved by two very handsome men, if I do so say so myself. Isn't that right, JD?"

"Yeah, Mama, two handsome men."

Katie offered a feeble smile and squeezed his hand. "I know, but my unsettled past and my fragile present are about to collide, and I'm concerned about the end result."

Unease shrouded his face. "How so?"

"I've worked hard to build a new life these last five years, but now I'm being pulled back into the location and life I never wanted to leave or lose in the first place. What if all I've worked to achieve falls apart?"

"We won't allow that to happen," Kyle said with determination.

Katie knew it wasn't a question of allowing it to happen, but a matter of surviving when it did. Four hours later, concern gave way to a forgotten awareness of belonging to this majestically haunting region. Colorful, imposing mountains of various shapes and sizes, lavishly covered and filled with evidence of bountiful life began to stir something long dormant inside.

Kyle patted her arm. "Nervous?"

"Yeah … but it's more." Taking a deep breath, she asked pensively, "Is it possible my heart never left this place?"

Kyle cast a quick glance her way. "Maybe that's why you've been reluctant to commit to a relationship."

"Maybe." She rolled down her window. "Even the air invigorates me."

Before Kyle could respond, JD asked the all-too-familiar question of all young travelers. "Are we there yet, Mama?"

"When I was a little girl, Mama told me that singing made the trip go faster."

"For real?" With that, JD began a recital of all his favorite songs. After a dozen or so and the fifteen verse of *Old McDonald*, Katie pointed to the road sign. "Take 25 south."

Stretching her hand, she patted her son's restless legs. "We are almost there." Giving Kyle directions and trying to keep JD calm kept her own anxiety in check until they turned into Wimberley Estates. "Look for 8214 Wimberley Lane. On the right, near the top of the hill."

The adults were quiet as they turned into the driveway, but not the child. "Wow, Mama. A rock house! Is this where you used to live?"

"I'm asking myself the same question, JD." Somehow, the stone house with its tile roof nestled on the five-acre wooded lot looked grander than she remembered. That was the moment a strange mixture of sadness and relief hit her … no one was home.

Kyle quickly exited and extracted JD from his seat and the car. "Let's stretch our legs while Mama checks out the place. Okay?"

Katie didn't budge until the sounds of her son's laughter and excitement pricked her curiosity. As she rounded the corner of the house, she ran into a wall of memories. Kyle was teaching JD how to pump the old tree swing to increase the height of his arc. "Look, Mama, I'm flying with the birds."

As she waved her approval, a mishmash of incidents involving that old swing surfaced. "Keep your eyes and ears open, Son. Folks say over two hundred varieties of birds, including the golden eagle, live in this area."

"Golden eagle?" Eyes as green as the hemlocks in the woods began to search the heavens. "I've never seen an eagle."

Her son's innocence and excitement provoked a smile. "Are those ropes safe, Kyle?" she asked as she neared the swing.

"Looks like they've been replaced in the last year or so." He studied her. "Are you okay?"

"Getting there. Having you and JD here helps."

Kyle wiped a stray tear. "That's my girl. How do we get in?"

"The folks always kept a spare under the small statue in the courtyard." She pointed to the one beside a grape mahonia bush. "Let's see if it's still there, JD."

"You two open up, and I'll get the luggage," Kyle said.

Katie took JD's hand in hers and guided the key into the slot. As they opened the door, a kaleidoscope of memories took over. Each one falling away only to yield to the next one forming.

Watching JD's delight with her home place put those replays in prospective. In forcing her to choose between them and him, her folks had unknowingly given her a glimpse into what love is and isn't. She didn't consider herself a saint or anything close, but the choice was never a choice for her. No one's favor or approval was worth the life of her child.

"Wow! This place is awesome, Mama." A systematic check of every room on the first floor and the second produced delighted sounds and instant approval. "Can we live here forever?"

"I doubt Mama left us the house, JD." That thought produced a surprising tinge of sadness.

"You and Mama don't need this house, JD. You're going to live with me in Roanoke. Remember?" replied the man loaded down with luggage. "Where do you want your belongings, Katie?"

A four bedroom, three-bath area connected to the foyer from the left and a formal dining room, kitchen with eating nook and hearth room to the right. An efficiency apartment connected via the hearth room and a two-car garage connected into the kitchen. The stairway and great room accounted for the large open space at the center rear of the house. Covered and grilling porches added to the outdoor area surrounding the patio and in-ground pool.

"Just set them in the hallway to the left, Kyle. I think I want JD's toy tub somewhere in the great room. It's centrally located."

After being convinced it was too cold for a swim, JD settled with his toys in the great room. Her architect boyfriend was preoccupied with his own diversions. "Your lifestyle never hinted your folks were people of means, Katie."

"Dad was a developer and investor who made good money, Kyle, but he didn't come close to the Vanderbilt type of wealth drawn to the area." Taking in the living space she hadn't seen in years, she added, "I loved this place from the day Dad showed me the plans until I was forced to leave. I still do."

He reached for a hand. "I'm concerned about your being here alone." His gaze held a measure of concern and a heightened level of desire. They had never discussed sex.

Hoping to distract him, she meandered toward the double doors that led to the covered porch and open patio on the back. As they scanned the fenced-in portion and beyond, Kyle stepped close. "I threw a change of clothes in the car."

Katie blushed. "Kyle, in case you're asking … giving me a ring didn't give you privileges."

Uncharacteristic of him up to this moment, he pushed the point. "So did JD's dad force himself on you or have your standards changed?"

Two flat hands smacked his chest and forcefully shoved him away. Fiery eyes charred any lingering desire. "That was uncalled for, Sir."

Hanging his head like a scolded puppy, he eased into a wicker chair on the porch. "You're right. The truth is … I'm jealous of JD's father."

His candidness defused her anger. "You have nothing to be jealous about."

His eyes shifted inside to JD's play area. "Obviously you didn't reject Jeremy. Why are you rejecting me?"

"Because I learned something important that night. Quick summary. The next man I make love to will be my husband." Placing her left hand on his arm, she added, "I'd say that would be you."

Gentle hands drew her onto his lap. "Then I hope you don't have to stay here long. We have a wedding to plan."

"I have no idea what the next few days have in store for me, Kyle." Katie slipped off his lap and reached for his hand. "Come on, I'll show you the rest of the place."

After the tour, Katie suggested they eat downtown. "It's too chilly for one of the sidewalk cafés, but I promise you won't be disappointed with the selection of eateries or the food." After their meal, she led them on a walking tour of the historic city and ended up at one of the gourmet chocolate shops.

"So you're a chocolate lover, huh?" Kyle asked as they walked back to his car.

"Isn't every woman?"

JD was walking between them. "Every boy too. Let's do that again, Mama."

It was dark when they returned. Kyle checked his watch as they walked inside. "I hate to leave, but I need to get on the road."

"You're going back tonight?" Katie's teapot pose always produced a Kyle smile.

"I had hoped to stay, but I respect your decision."

"Have you forgotten there are three bedrooms upstairs?"

He pulled her close. "Honey, when we sleep under the same roof, it won't be in separate bedrooms." His kiss left no doubt.

Katie squirmed out of his reach. "Kyle …" The next time he reached for her, she playfully scooted a chair between them. "You definitely need to leave."

She scurried into the kitchen area, located a scrap piece of paper, and jotted down the home phone number. "Here, call me when you get home … regardless of the time."

"Yes, Ma'am. Any other orders?"

"Don't forget your little buddy."

Kyle strolled into the great room where JD was playing. "I'm leaving, Son."

The kid sprang from the floor and leaped into welcoming arms.

"You be a good boy for mama, okay?"

"Okay, Daddy." They shared a hug and JD returned to his cars.

Kyle motioned for Katie to follow him out. "Are you concerned about JD's dad?"

A nervous expression manifest. "Yeah, him and the rest of the town." Two tears escaped and she melted as he enfolded her in his protective embrace. "Thank you for driving us down."

"My pleasure. Promise me this ring will remind you of the man in Roanoke who adores you and that son of yours."

Admiring the object of their discussion, she added, "This is an impressive reminder."

"It was meant to be." He hesitated a second and then hugged her. "Katie, I know you don't love me the way I love you … yet … but you do love me … don't you?"

Pangs of empathy hit. "I do, Kyle, but it is a quiet love, not a raging fire. Is that enough?"

He kissed the top of her head. "For now."

She walked him to his car and felt his absence as he drove away. As she closed the front door, she saw the lights of another vehicle in the driveway. One glance and Katie braced herself. Aunt Edith. Before she dashed outside, she stuck her head in the great room. "JD, stay put. Mama needs to talk to someone privately."

He barely acknowledged her request. Katie hurried out the door, secured her position on the top step and watched as Aunt Edith spent several minutes surveying the garage and driveway area.

"Did I see a Mercedes pull out of this driveway?"

"Now, Auntie, how am I supposed to know what you saw?"

"Still have a smart mouth, don't you? I'm trying to figure out how you got here, Katie."

"A friend." Edith's once-overs always made Katie want to wallow in a mud hole and put chewing gum in her hair. Today she added hiding her engagement ring.

"You've filled out nicely. Hope you brought some proper clothes, and for heaven's sake, do something with that wild, unruly hair besides braid it."

The meddlesome relative glanced towards the house. "Did you bring that boy of yours or are you going to keep him hidden the rest of his life?"

Katie stiffened her posture and acid leaked into her tone. "Is there something you need, Aunt Edith?"

The older woman bristled. "Well, I assumed since I'm the only family you have left, you'd be glad to see me."

With a hardness that had developed over the years, Katie stared at the woman who reminded her of her dad though she was her mother's sister. "I've lived without a family for the last five years and unless I'm having a memory lapse, I believe that included you, Auntie."

That same vein in her forehead began to bulge as stone-cold eyes zeroed in on their target. "Well, I never! Young Lady, your dad wouldn't have sent you away if you hadn't gotten yourself pregnant. I agreed with his decision."

"What a shock!" Katie said mockingly as her hands covered her heart.

"You are an insolent girl. Always have been. I tried to warn Edgar about you in the beginning, but he wouldn't listen." Edith tugged at the bottom of her suit coat then fiddled with the broach on her lapel.

"Good evening, Aunt Edith." Katie walked into the house, closed the door and slid to the floor. *Who needs family?*

JD ran to her side. "What's wrong, Mama?"

Ahh, here was her family. Katie held back the tears but opened her arms. "Nothing a hug from you won't cure."

Little arms squeezed her tight. "Is it all better now, Mama?"

"All better, Son."

After JD returned to his toy station, Katie located the local phone directory. Her finger trembled as she traced down the Ws. Did he still live in the area? Was his name and number listed? Was he married? Her breath caught. *Jeremy Webster.*

A few unidentified creatures joined the swarm of butterflies that had invaded her digestive tract since the phone call this morning. Memories crowded her mind as she listened to the rings echoing on her end of the line. After counting five, she heard his voice. *You have reached Jeremy Webster. Please leave a number and a message. I will be in touch.* Her heart was in her throat ... which made breathing and speaking challenging.

"Huh, Jeremy ... this is Katie. Guess you heard ... about mom. I, uh ... I just arrived in town and am staying at her place."

She took a deep breath. "I was wondering ... if we could talk ... tonight if possible." She left her mom's number and hung up.

Her frantic quest for a brown paper bag proved as unproductive as a desperate search for ginger ale. After rummaging through three medicine cabinets, she did find a bottle of *Tums* and quickly downed a handful.

Clammy hands, a galloping heart and beasts in the digestive tract ... all because of Jeremy Webster. What could she do to occupy her mind? Vehicles. Check out the vehicles.

Wouldn't you know it? The passage door from the kitchen to the garage was dragging. Pulling and tugging produced no success. After bracing a foot on the doorframe and putting all of her nervous energy into an all-out tug, she tumbled backwards as the door broke loose. A loud *ouch* escaped.

JD ran in. "Whatcha doing, Mama?"

"Checking out our mode of transportation, Son." She picked herself up ... ignoring the pain in her backside.

JD's eyes lit up when he spied the big Dodge truck. "Whose is that, Mama?"

"Not sure who will end up with all this stuff, JD. Until we find out, I plan to use it."

"Can we go for a ride … now?" He was circling the vehicle as if it were the eighth wonder of the world.

Boys and their toys. Before she could answer, the phone rang. She grabbed her drooling son and hurried back in the house. "If you'll go play with your pretend trucks for a few minutes, we'll go for a ride in the real one tomorrow. Mama needs to take this call."

"Oh, boy!" And the new big truck enthusiast disappeared.

Katie took a deep breath and reached for the phone. "Hel-lo."

"Katie?"

One word and every wall she had erected came crashing down. Every tear she had refused to shed found an outlet and they seemed determined to keep pace with her runaway heart. "Yeah … it's me."

Silence reigned on both ends of the line. Katie was struggling to breathe and hold the contents of her last meal down. Scared to speak up, but more afraid of the repercussions if she didn't, Katie took the lead. "Please … don't hang up, Jeremy."

An angry voice responded. "Hang up? What if I just drop off the face of the earth for five years?" He was incensed. "Where have you been, Katie Williams?"

"Me disappear? I believe you chose that option first, Jeremy Webster." Now there were two angry voices. It felt good to get it off her chest after all this time.

Silence returned and Katie refused to say another word. If he didn't want to come tonight, then he could find out about his son about the same time everyone else did.

A calmer voice responded. "Obviously, we need to talk. I'll be there in fifteen minutes."

That sounded like the Jeremy she had known and memories of their two-year, secret courtship began playing on the silver screen of her mind. "Okay," she offered with more anxiety than anger this time.

"Katie?"

"Yeah?"

"Promise you won't disappear."

"I'll be here."

Three

A couple of swine joined the party in her stomach, and they were uprooting everything she had stuffed down since the day he walked out of her life. She ran to the bathroom.

"Mama, are you sick?"

"A little, but I'll be okay." Within minutes of JD's exit, she began hurling. When the heaves lessened, she settled on the side of the tub with a damp washcloth on her forehead. Too soon, she heard the door chimes.

After rinsing her mouth and checking her appearance, she nervously approached the door. On the other side stood JD's father. Her hand trembled as she turned the knob.

Heaven help her. She had an overpowering urge to leap into his arms, but her body froze. Neither moved nor spoke. Both stared. When Katie noted a slight upturn of the right side of his mouth, she wondered if she might be wearing evidence of her bathroom visit. Was he overcome by the odor? The more she thought about it, the more she considered the possibilities. Were fragments hanging from her braid? Her hand began to work its way down the black plait.

Were remnants clinging to her clothes? With eyes still glued to his, her hand moved over the front of her shirt.

When Katie mustered enough courage to speak, her stomach mistook the open mouth for permission to finish the purging assignment. Before she could turn away, she littered his clothes. The assaulted man pulled her to the side and moved her thick braid out of the path.

When it seemed nothing remained, Jeremy offered his handkerchief. "Interesting greeting, Katie. Are you trying to tell me something?"

Her eyes swept up and down his freshly glazed attire only to land on his dazzling emerald eyes again. Dare she open her mouth?

"Are you okay?" he asked.

A little more confident her words now had the right-of-way, Katie ventured an answer. "Mama's death and coming back home have been unsettling, Jeremy Webster, but *you* are the cause of this embarrassing greeting."

The soiled man allowed a bold smile to escape. "Can't remember ever having that effect on anyone before." He swept a stray strand of hair off her face and allowed his fingers to linger. "It's not my stomach that has been in turmoil since your call, Katie."

His touch ... his voice ... those words ... that look ...

"Mama, are you sick again?" JD was standing in the open doorway.

Jeremy's head jerked toward the sound of the man-child.

Innocent, matching green eyes met his. "Hi, Mister. Who are you?"

Jeremy stared at the child and then his mother. "Katie? Is this ... our ...?"

His voice trailed off as the woman knelt in front of the boy who bore his image. "Mama and her friend need to get cleaned up, JD. Why don't you make one of your play dough monsters for our visitor?"

JD studied the man. "Hey, your skin matches mine. Mama says it's the prettiest God makes."

Stunned and speechless, Jeremy watched his miniature likeness scamper away.

"Now you know why I called."

When he didn't respond, she seized his hand and led him to a bathroom. "I can't believe I upchucked on you."

Katie watched as the shocking reality of having a son took root. Bewilderment gave way to a scary, wild look that hinted of a serious reaction. He seized her shoulders and shook her body until her head bobbed. She burped ... loudly. "Forget about the stinking clothes, Katie. I'm trying to take in the fact that we ... have ... a son."

Using all her strength, she unsuccessfully tried to disengage his hands from her body. "Unless you want to add whatever's left in my stomach to your attire, I suggest you calm down and unhand me."

Jeremy threw his hands in the air and began pacing like a caged animal. "Calm down? Within three minutes, you have covered me with the foulest vomit I've ever smelled and presented me with the most beautiful four-year-old boy I've ever seen. Woman, calm is not possible at this moment."

He abruptly moved to the sink, grabbed a washcloth and began attacking the remnants of her rejected food with the vengeance of a ravenous dog while muttering in Pig Latin.

Katie had forgotten their Pig Latin days. When he glared at her in the mirror, she leaned closer to be sure those were real tears rolling down his cheeks. "Jeremy, are you okay?" He turned to face her. Yep, his green pools had sprung a couple of leaks.

"Okay? Obviously you've forgotten your Pig Latin or you would be aware that *okay* was not among the list of terms I used to describe my feelings and thoughts at this moment."

He threw the cloth down and started pacing again. "How in the Sam Hill did you think I'd be? Pleased that you disappeared for five years without a word? Oozing with gratitude that you've kept my son a secret? Okay, you ask. Woman, I am so angry and confused at this moment I don't know how I am. Part of me wants to hug you and never let go. The other part is tempted to haul you off to jail and throw away the key. I cannot believe you did this to me ... to us ... to him."

The stormy look in his eyes convinced her he was leaning more towards jail than a hug. "Look, I know this has been a shock. Why don't you go home and come back after you've cleaned up and calmed down?" When he attached his hands to her shoulders again, she thought she saw faint images of iron bars in his eyes.

"First thing I have to do is cancel a date. Where's the closest phone?" he asked as he released her.

Moving out of his reach, she pointed to the bedroom nightstand. He called someone named Valerie or Vanessa and explained that something had come up. "No, it is not work related. It's personal. You'll just have to trust me." His eyes had Katie nailed in her spot. "Huh? Yeah, love you too." Katie was guessing the "V" person was not happy.

Jeremy hung up, moved back into Katie's space and resumed his non-affectionate hand to shoulder grip. "Me leave? Not on your life. I'm not going anywhere or letting you out of my sight until I get some answers. Do you understand?"

Katie stiffened to keep from melting. His touch was still magical. "Well, I'm going to take a shower and change into some clean clothes. I suggest you alter your declaration a smidgeon and consider how best to get yourself cleaned up."

Jeremy didn't bat an eye. "You have ten minutes or I'll haul you out. And I'll be watching the door."

She shook his hands loose and heaved a piece of her luggage on the bed. "I don't remember you being so bossy and unreasonable." After snatching some clothes, she headed for the shower.

He seized her arm. "Add angry to that list. If your mom hadn't died, I still wouldn't know." Jeremy's right hand slid down her left arm and stopped when it landed on the ring. "From the looks of that thing, you're making plans for my son that don't include me." He leaned in until they were nose to nose. "I am furious with you, Katie."

The hurt behind his anger was tugging at her fragile composure. "I'm sorry, Jeremy."

"Sorry? That's all you have to say?" He stormed out of the room.

After showering and changing clothes, Katie exited the bathroom to find Jeremy sitting on the bed … wearing a towel. His athletic legs and muscular, bare chest threw her off guard. "What do you think you're doing?"

"*Our son* showed me the washer for my clothes and the adjoining shower for my body. He and I decided a towel was better than nothing. Any better ideas?"

Planting her hands on her hips, she faced the half-clothed man. "Did I forget to tell you to make yourself at home?"

Lifting a set of cuffs dangling from his wrists, he exaggerated his officer pose. "Don't get sassy with me, Katie. You're already on thin ice."

About that time, JD showed up. "Look at my monster, Mama."

Examining his offering carefully gave her some recoup time. "I think that's the best one you've ever made." She scooped him off his feet. "Let's go see what else you've created."

A firm hand to the shoulder stopped her. "I believe he made that for me."

JD held it out. "I did."

Jeremy traced the clay creature's arms and legs and smiled at the oversized head. "Mind if I take it home?"

"Sure, Mister. Want me to make him a brother so he won't get lonesome? I don't have a brother, and sometimes I get lonely."

Jeremy's expression softened. "I'd like that very much."

JD squirmed out of Katie's arms and disappeared. When she attempted to follow, Jeremy blocked her way. "Why have you kept him a secret?"

She pushed and shoved her way around his athletic body. "Exactly when and how was I supposed to tell you, Jeremy? *You* disappeared."

Unable to contain his exasperation any longer, his voice echoed throughout the house. "How was I supposed to know you were pregnant?"

JD charged into the room. "Why are you yelling at my mama?

I'll tell Kyle and he'll beat you up." His eyes were challenging and his stance was protective.

Jeremy fell to his knees beside the boy. "Yelling was wrong and I'm sorry, JD, but your mama has kept a very important secret from me."

JD scrutinized the two. "Why did you do that, Mama? And why are you crying?"

Katie's eyes fastened on Jeremy. "I didn't think you cared."

Unbelief framed the man's face. "Not care, Katie?" His fingers gently wiped her tears. "You knew I was in love with you."

Those words and his nearness were her undoing. She fell against his chest and sobbed. "Then why did you walk away?"

JD was hugging a leg as Jeremy embraced her. "We need to talk, but right now I'd like for this young man to know who I am." He lifted her chin. "Is that okay with you?"

A nod was all she could manage.

"Let's go to the great room," Jeremy suggested.

Katie had to put some space between them. His bare chest and her exposed heart were wreaking havoc with her will to resist him and be true to her commitment to Kyle. She reached for their son. "JD, mama has a surprise for you."

The kid began looking around. "Where is it?"

"Very close."

Jeremy sat on a footstool close to the play area. Katie and JD settled on the loveseat nearby. "Little Buddy, can you tell me your name?" Jeremy's voice was unsteady.

"JD Webster," he shared with pride.

Surprise lit up Jeremy's face. "Your last name is Webster?"

"Yeah, that's my daddy's name. What's yours?"

"My first name is Jeremiah." He watched the boy's reaction.

Turning to Katie he asked, "Isn't that one of my names, Mama?"

Nods would have to do until her emotions settled.

Jeremy fingered one of his son's soft curls. "My middle name is Daniel. Any idea what yours is?"

JD sought confirmation. "Is it Daniel, Mama?"

Tears accompanied the nod this time.

Jeremy was fighting his own. "Can you guess what my last name is, JD?"

The lad shook his head.

"Webster. My name is Jeremiah Daniel Webster."

A confused look clouded the boy's face. Silence reigned momentarily as all three took a deep, collective breath. "Mama, is that my name too?"

Jeremy choked. Katie knelt in front of the man and beside her son. "Yes ... it is." Her voice wavered as warm tears wore a path down her cheeks. "JD ... Jeremy ... is your daddy."

The surprised boy studied the emotional man. "Are you sad that you're my daddy?"

"Oh, no, JD. Knowing you are my son is wonderful news. My only sadness is that I've missed four years of your life."

JD hugged him. "We found him, Mama. We finally found him." Suddenly his little face wrinkled. "What about Kyle? He's going to be my daddy. You promised. Can I have two?"

Katie couldn't respond. The stomach monsters were back. "Excuse me." She rushed to the bathroom with spasms that doubled her over. Thirty minutes later, she quietly slipped into the playroom to find father and son in the floor building a Lincoln Log fort.

Jeremy's gaze met hers. "Mind if I stay until his bedtime?"

How could he be so calm? "That's fine."

She went to the hearth room to give them time alone. An hour later JD crawled in her lap. "Can I go to bed now?"

Jeremy's tears escaped again when JD thanked God for helping them find his daddy. After goodnights and a promise to come back tomorrow, the two adults retired to the hearth room. "Tell me about Kyle."

As best she could, Katie explained his role in their lives. "He and Aunt Bea are the only real friends I've had since I left Asheville."

He joined her on the sofa and reached for her left hand. "That engagement ring is not from a friend, Katie."

She held out the ring and managed a smile. "It is a bit extravagant, isn't it? Poor rich boy. He simply doesn't know how to be everyday ordinary. That's one of the reasons I've been slow about saying yes." Her gaze moved to Jeremy's green eyes. "He loves my son and I do care for him."

"Is he white or black?"

"White."

"How does he feel about having a biracial child?"

Her brows puckered. "You think I would get involved with a man who has trouble with JD?" Her questioning look gradually morphed into a teasing one. "What I'm having trouble with right now is you and that towel." She led the way to the laundry room and transferred his wet clothes into the dryer.

"Sorry, but I've had more important things on my mind." After adding a couple of logs to the fire, he faced her. "Katie, what happened to you?"

"What happened?" She had to remember to keep her voice down. "*You* stopped all contact after the night JD was conceived. Three weeks later, my morning sickness announced our indiscretion to my folks. Somehow, they knew it was your baby. When I refused an abortion, they packed everything I owned and hauled me off to Roanoke. They died waiting for me to give up custody of JD."

"Why didn't you call my folks when you didn't hear from me?" His voice was heavy with regret.

"I took your silence as rejection. Calling your folks never crossed my mind."

"God, forgive me." He knelt in front of her. "Katie, I went home that night and told my folks I was going to marry you. It was your eighteen birthday and I knew your folks couldn't stop us."

She looked at him through her tears. "Why am I just now hearing this?"

"Because my folks convinced me your parents would never accept me, our marriage or our children. I knew that our lives as a racially-mixed couple would be hard at best, and I loved you too much to alienate you from your family."

Her swollen, red eyes filled with fire. "Didn't you think you at least owed me an explanation? Or the chance to choose for myself?" She rose and walked to the back door that offered a private view of the enclosed pool area and the woods beyond.

Jeremy approached. "Katie, I knew if I made any kind of contact, I'd lose my resolve. Had I known you were pregnant, I'd have fought the devil himself for you and our baby."

Slowly she faced him. "I knew that. But tell me, Jeremy, how do you think a woman feels when a man marries her because she is carrying his child? I wanted to find out if you would asked if you didn't know. And guess what? You didn't. I can do without that kind of love. Thank you."

"God, I was so wrong! Every day we were apart proved how much. By the time I realized I had made a huge mistake, Katie, you had disappeared and your folks were as silent as the grave. That's when I joined the Marines."

His nearness and confession were toying with her commitment to Kyle. "Tell me about *Veronica*."

"Her name is Valerie." He moved to the fireplace. "I joined the Asheville Police Department when I got out of the Marines. Your dad died shortly afterwards. Your absence at his funeral convinced me I'd never see you again. That hopelessness set me up for Valerie. Our wedding is scheduled for December 26."

"Is she white?"

"No. My folks persuaded me that life would be easier for all of us if I married someone of color."

An adrenaline surge bought Katie out of her seat. "Looks like prejudice lives on both sides of the *race* tracks." She slapped away the hand that reached to calm her.

"Mom and Dad knew the trouble you and I had during our dating years, Katie. They were just trying to make life a little easier."

"Let's get honest, Jeremy. Bottom line … you walked away from me because I was a white girl." Angry tears were cascading down her cheeks as she marched towards the front door. "It's time for you to leave."

Ignoring her attempts to end the conversation, he grabbed the poker and rearranged the logs. "Not because *you* were white, but because your *white* parents hated me. I didn't want to rip you away from them. There is a difference."

"Well, guess what. It happened anyway and I chose my son over them, Jeremy. I would have chosen you if given the chance. Please leave."

"Like this?" He modeled his towel.

She scurried to the laundry room, retrieved his clothes and threw them at him. "Here. Get dressed. Whatshername and Kyle would not approve of your apparel."

"Katie, we can't change the past, but we can redirect our futures. I'd marry you tonight if you'd agree."

Her head jerked in his direction. "Tonight? Have you forgotten about Kyle and *Valencia*? Does she even know I exist?"

He rubbed his bare feet back and forth on the hardwood floor. "Her name is Valerie. No, I haven't told her about you or us."

Hands flew to her hips as words were forming in her head. "I would have married you then, but not now. I've made a commitment to someone else and so have you." Before walking out of the room she added, "Lock the door on your way out."

By the time he finished dressing, Katie had disappeared. A search of the more public rooms of the house was futile. Where was the woman? Surely, she was not upstairs. He headed towards the bedroom area and peeked into JD's room. She was kneeling by his bed … weeping.

He leaned against the doorframe and watched. Seeing her again had resurrected every feeling he had ever had for her. Discovering they had a son was rocking his world. What was he going to do? When Katie rose and brushed by without a word, he lingered. Pondering. Praying.

Fighting the urge to grab a pillow and sleep on the floor beside his son, he wandered back to the warmth of the fire. Katie joined him sometime later.

"Jeremy, you need to go home."

"Easy said, Katie, but seeing you again and meeting our son has me totally disoriented. I'm afraid you and JD are figments of my imagination or some wonderful dream I'm having, and if I leave, the two of you will vanish into thin air."

"I promise we won't."

He couldn't keep his eyes off her. The woman was more beautiful than the girl he fell in love with. "Have you thought about the town's reaction to JD the next two days?"

She lowered her eyelids and rubbed her neck. "Yeah, I figure it'll be rough."

"I can't allow you to face them alone. I'd like to accompany you and JD, and for those too blind to figure it out, I want them to know he is our son. Are you okay with that?"

She smirked and reached for the local newspaper. "I'll bet *Vannah* will put an announcement in the paper the next day and hire the pep band to celebrate that news. If you were afraid to tell her you dated a white girl, how will you tell her about our son?"

"Her name is Valerie and she definitely presents a problem." When she dared to look at him again, he pleaded, "Give me another chance, Katie."

She fingered the ring. "I can't do that to Kyle."

Jeremy was not budging. "Do you love him or did you say yes because of JD's attachment?"

"I do love him, and didn't I hear you repeat those words to *Vanita?*"

He took a deep breath. "Let's admit it. There are different kinds of love, and we've settled for less than we've already experienced." A teasing smile etched his face. "Can't bring yourself to say her name, can you?"

Katie began to tremble and pain equal to a wounded fellow soldier was evident on her face. "Did you asked your parents' permission before you proposed? Did they give her their blessing? Did they encourage you to buy her a ring? Are they excited about your wedding? Is she pregnant with your baby?" She buried her face in her hands and sobbed.

Jeremy sobered. How blind could he be? He gently enclosed her in his arms. "Oh, Katie. I have grievously sinned against you." Her pain became his. "Father, this woman has deep, raw wounds and the fault lies at my feet. I didn't honor her or You the last time we were together. Then I walked away in the name of love. What a joke! I left a trail of rejection and betrayal for her to walk ... alone. I marvel that You chose that night to begin the weaving of our son.

"I was wrong to listen to the fears of my folks, and I was wrong to walk away." When Jeremy paused to gain control of his own emotions and voice, he felt Katie relax some.

"Jesus, she is wounded beyond my imagination, but not Yours. You know all about rejection. You understand being forsaken and abandoned. You suffered the pain of prejudice. Your own mother lived with the shame and judgment of a being a pregnant, unwed mother. Unlike me, You never walked away, rejected or betrayed her."

She was wiping her eyes on the sleeve of his shirt.

"I can't undo what's been done, Lord, but I can and do repent and ask forgiveness ... from You and her." He lifted her chin and waited for their eyes to connect. "Katie, I was wrong about so many things. Can you forgive me?"

Her eyes delved into his soul before she nodded and buried her face in his chest again. "Father, let this night be the beginning of healing for Katie ... and our relationship ... whatever it's supposed to look like. In Jesus name."

He stayed quiet until her tears slowed and her trembling ceased. When she pulled away, he reached for her hands. "I'll be breaking my engagement regardless of your decision, Katie. And no, Valerie isn't carrying my baby."

She lifted her gaze from their hands to his face. "What are you saying?"

He gently kissed each salty eye. "That I'm still hopelessly in love with you."

Her inquisitive eyes were alive. "What about *Velvetta*?"

Jeremy laughed. "Have I told you green is one of your better colors?"

"You won't be laughing when you explain to *Miss Vendetta* about our son and your desire to marry his white mother."

He kissed her cheek and headed for the door. "What time do you need to be at the funeral home in the morning?"

"Ten o'clock."

"I'll be here early to help with JD."

"Goodnight, Jeremy."

"Night, Katie."

Four

As promised, Jeremy arrived early the next morning. Casting an approving smile in Katie's direction, he hoisted JD on his shoulders. "Your mama is a fine looking woman, and you are a handsome young man, Son."

JD leaned close to his ear. "That's what Kyle says. Do all daddies talk like that?"

A soberness shaded Jeremy's face as he shifted the boy into his arms. "Son, Kyle is not your daddy."

"He wants to be and I like him."

Jeremy was at a loss. His heart protested, but he had to accept the fact that unless he could change Katie's mind, it was going to happen.

"Mama says you and I are going to spend the day together." The boy hugged him. "I like you 'cause we look alike."

Jeremy's heart was so full he thought it might burst. "That's because you are my son. Is it okay if I tell folks that today?"

The kid beamed. "Is it, Mama?"

She straightened JD's collar and cast Jeremy a knowing glance. "I think they'll figure that out regardless." Looking between the two, she added, "This is the day the world will meet our fine son, Jeremy. I'm glad you're here for that. What about work?"

"Off today and tomorrow." He snaked an arm around Katie's waist. "Starting today I'm going to make up for all the days and years you and JD faced life alone." Memories of last night still haunted him.

Thinking she was favorably responsive, he kissed her lightly on the lips. She pushed away but made no verbal protest.

"The Webster men have your back today, Katie, but you need to know … it's your heart I'm after."

"You were sole owner at one time, Sir. Did you talk with *Vanity* last night?"

"It wasn't the right time. I'll figure out a way to break it to her tonight."

Katie shot him a *you've-got-to-be-kidding* look. "Good luck." She tossed him her mom's car keys. "Do you mind driving?"

After picking up JD, he opened the door for Katie. "Mind? Spending time with you and JD moved to the top of my priority list yesterday. Except for the circumstances, Katie, there's nowhere I'd rather be."

As the threesome entered the Turner Funeral home, several employees expressed their sympathy and a couple cast questionable glances. Jeremy proudly introduced JD and visited with employees while Katie spoke with Isaac.

The man was kind. "Do you want an open or closed casket, Katie? Your mother couldn't decide."

"Keep it closed, Isaac."

He nodded towards the man at his side. "Take care of that, will you, Arthur?"

Glancing towards Jeremy and JD, Isaac smiled. "Looks like God used your mom's death to bring your own family together, Katie. Life out of death. Has a familiar ring, doesn't it?"

Katie fingered Kyle's ring. "How much have folks heard or figured out, Isaac?"

"Most folks guessed your leaving had something to do with

Jeremy. When he returned from his tour of duty and you didn't show up for Edgar's funeral, people assumed you were never coming back. They'll be surprised to see you and the boy."

"Dad told Mom he didn't want me at his funeral."

Pity or compassion ... maybe both ... radiated from Isaac's face. "I'm afraid folks have misjudged you."

Uncomfortable with the implications, they turned to watch father and son. "Jeremy didn't know about JD until yesterday, Isaac."

The kind soul acknowledged the approaching duo. "Mighty fine boy you have there, Jeremy."

"That he is."

Isaac dismissed himself and quickly retrieved a rather large envelope. "Your mom's will and other information you'll need, Katie."

A sweaty hand accepted the first physical contact from either parent since June 1990. "Thanks, Isaac."

"You'll find everything in order, Katie. If you have any questions, just give me a call."

After concluding arrangements with Isaac, the threesome proceeded to Martha's car. "How are you holding up?" Jeremy asked.

"I'm numb. In reality, I grieved losing Mom and Dad the nine months I carried JD. Today I'm more concerned with folks' response to him than I am her death. Is that wrong?"

"It's understandable." He reached for a hand. "Would you consider lunch at the Carriage House? JD and I are hungry."

Katie stopped in her tracks. "Jeremy?"

He placed JD in his car seat and then helped her in the passenger's side. "No more shame and hiding, Katie. Some will hold our past sins against us, and others will frown on our crossing racial lines. I choose to forgive them like God has forgiven me and refuse to surrender to their prejudice.

A troubled look clouded her face. "Jeremy, apart from our obvious indiscretion and the racial issue, both of us are engaged ... to other people. Don't you think you are inviting gossip?"

"Honey, apart from the fact that I plan to break my engagement tonight, JD is my son and you are his mother. Surely Valerie and Kyle wouldn't object to a public meal together."

Katie allowed a faint smile to emerge. "I am hungry."

The Carriage House experience had the female on pins and needles, but the male was unruffled. Katie was focusing on the menu when she caught a glimpse of a woman making a scene skirting tables and brushing by patrons. Her heart leaped. It was an old friend. After they shared a hug, Jeremy pulled out the fourth chair for Charlotte.

"Girlfriend, I had given up hope of ever see you again. Where have you been?"

"My folks kicked me out." Katie made the introductions. "Charlotte, this is my son, JD."

Jeremy interrupted, "Excuse me. This is *our* son."

Charlotte's non-condemning smile said it all. "Hi, JD."

Big green eyes sparkled. "Are you my mama's friend?"

"Forever and always, JD."

Turning to his father, she asked, "You didn't know?"

"Not until yesterday."

At that moment, her eyes caught a glimpse of Katie's diamond. Her eyebrows shot up as she reached for the ring. "Who robbed Tiffany's?"

Katie tried to withdraw her hand. "My fiancé lives in Roanoke."

Charlotte hung on and carefully examined the ring. "That thing screams of extravagance, Katie." Then she studied her friends. "Hmmm."

"Don't give me that look, Charlotte. Jeremy is engaged to *Whoosit*. Remember?"

Jeremy grinned. "Charlotte knows Valerie. Any tips on breaking an engagement with the least amount of collateral damage?"

Charlotte shook her head in amazement. "This close to your wedding? Because of a white woman? And a son? Only in your dreams, Officer. I suggest wearing your flak jacket." She grinned playfully. "You two always did make the soap operas boring. Can't wait to hear how this episode turns out."

Katie's eyebrows met in the middle. "I'm glad you find our

dilemma humorous, because life on this side of the big screen is a bit overwhelming."

Charlotte snatched a napkin and commandeered Jeremy's pen. "Add me to your phone list. I don't want to miss anything." She hugged Katie. "I don't know about the man in Roanoke, Katie, but it's plain as the nose on your face this one is still in love with you." Nodding in the direction of the Webster men she added, "Don't see how you could separate them again."

After an enjoyable meal and time together, Jeremy paid the bill and his family-for-the-night walked to the car. "How are your folks taking the news about breaking things off with *Valium?*"

He grinned as he buckled JD into his chair. "You are creative." A more serious expression replaced his smile. "They've asked my forgiveness and hope to have an opportunity to seek yours. They are encouraging me to right the wrongs done to you and JD, Katie."

"Daddy, are you going to live with us? Kyle said we were going to live with him when we get back to Roanoke."

Jeremy glanced at Katie. "That's up to your mama, Son."

Katie turned on the radio to keep from discussing the subject.

JD was asleep by the time they turned into Wimberley Estates. Jeremy carried him to his bedroom. After pouring two glasses of sweet, mint tea and grabbing her mom's will, Katie settled on the sofa.

A soft rap on the back door evoked sweet memories. Only one person ever used the back door. Mrs. Carpenter. The woman's sunny disposition and her chocolate treats had brightened many a day.

Mrs. Carpenter's clear hazel eyes danced when Katie opened the door. "I remembered how much you liked my chocolate desserts," she said as she held out a nine-inch pie that would make the prize baker in town jealous.

Katie hugged the sweet lady. "I've missed you and your delicious treats, Mrs. C. Wasn't it you who told me chocolate makes everything better?"

"Yeah, and I haven't changed my mind," she said as she carried the pie into the kitchen.

Jeremy walked in on the friendly exchange. "Hi, Mrs. Carpenter. Good to see you."

The neighbor deliberated a few seconds. "Well now, Officer, I hope you're not here on official business."

Jeremy chuckled. "No, just visiting Katie and JD."

"JD?"

Katie intervened. "JD is our son, Mrs. Carpenter."

A smile of understanding lit up her face. "So that's why your folks sent you away?"

Katie was back to the nods.

"Shame on them. It's not as though God ran out of forgiveness or grace." The wrinkles in her forehead deepened as she studied the two. "What about Valerie, Son?"

"We've got ourselves a tricky situation for sure, Mrs. Carpenter. Any advice for breaking an engagement?"

She rolled her eyes and smiled. "Ooo-eee, Child, this situation would challenge *Dear Abby*. My only advice is *don't put it off*."

"I'm working on it."

She turned to leave. "Can't wait to meet JD."

Katie walked her to the door. "I'll bring him over soon."

"It's good to have you home, Katie."

"Thanks again for the pie," Katie said as she watched the elderly neighbor open the gate her dad had installed between the two properties when he put up the fence.

Jeremy handed her a dessert plate graced with a slice of kindness. "Did you talk to Kyle last night?"

"Of course. Shouldn't you be spending time with *Whatshername* instead of sharing chocolate pie with an old flame?"

"Old flame? Sweetheart, the old flame has ignited a forest fire." He studied her as the delicacy tantalized his taste buds. "I think there is a raging fire behind your smoke screen too, Katie. The sooner we deal with Kyle and Valerie, the better."

Katie stiffened. "Speak for yourself. I respect the man who gave me this ring, and I have no intention of destroying his trust, Jeremy."

He placed a finger under her chin. "So tell me how trust without love feels, Katie."

She did not blink. "Safer than love without trust, Jeremy."

Unbelief radiated from his face. "Katie, after our talks, you still plan to marry Kyle?"

"Yes, but first, I have to bury Mama. Or have you forgotten why I'm here in the first place?"

Jeremy softened. "Forgive me." He hesitated and then turned to leave. I'll see myself out."

Thoughts of Jeremy Webster and Kyle Butler kept Katie tossing and turning to the point she couldn't determine if the sound she heard was real or in her troubled sleep. Her alarm clock registered 2:48 a.m. Must have been a dream. She fluffed her pillow and pulled up the covers only to hear the sound again. That was no dream. Someone was at the front door. That was scary.

Snatching her housecoat, she grabbed a poker from the fireplace set before checking the peephole. There stood her fiancé with a garment bag in one hand and a gym bag in the other. A click of the latches cleared the opening between them. "Do you know what time it is?" she asked with a mix of relief and curiosity.

"Do you mind if we have this discussion inside?"

Katie stepped aside as the morning caller glided into her house, hung the clothes bag in the foyer closet, set his bag inside and took in her apparel with weary, but approving eyes.

"Hmmm. I like the morning you," he said as he tilted her chin and kissed her rather passionately.

She pushed back. "Explain yourself, please."

"The more I thought about it, the more I knew I couldn't let you do this funeral thing by yourself. Soooo, I worked late and finished today's work at ten last night. I'm hoping your offer for an upstairs room is still open." He glanced at her clothing. "Unless you've changed your mind about my sleeping arrangements."

"No change, Sir."

Little feet came pounding into the area. "Kyle!"

Open arms greeted the youngster. "Hello, Buddy. I've missed you."

They hugged and shared some man chatter before JD leaked the news. "I have two daddies now."

Kyle tousled the lad's loose curls. "I'm glad you met your other daddy, Son. Have you been taking care of mama?"

"Uh-huh, and Daddy helps. He hugs and kisses her ... same as you do. Is that okay?"

Though Kyle's face turned beet red, he managed to keep his voice calm. "Hey, it's too early to be up. What if I tuck you in and we'll talk more when the sun comes up."

JD glanced at Katie. "He'll be here when you wake, Son."

A mischievous grin filled his young face. "You wanna kiss Mama, dontcha?"

The upset man relaxed some. "Smart boy. Come on. Let's get you back to bed."

When he returned he took a seat on the steps and patted the space beside him. "You have some explaining to do."

"It's not as bad as it sounds, Kyle."

"Pray tell me what is good about it, Katie."

She placed her left hand on his knee. "I'm still wearing your ring."

Kyle's arms enclosed her. "Then he needs to leave my girl alone. I'm the jealous type ... in case you didn't know."

Before she could answer, he kissed her possessively. "Now, if you don't mind, I'd like for you to guard those lips when I'm not around." He fingered the ring. "In case the man is blind, this is a *no trespassing* sign, Katie. Do I need to explain the ground rules?"

"I'll take care of it, Kyle. I promise."

Seemingly satisfied, he changed the subject. "I have a surprise waiting for you in Roanoke."

Concern registered on Katie's face. "What have you done?"

"I'm getting things ready for us." His head was resting on her shoulders.

"Kyle, go to bed. You are exhausted."

He didn't argue. "Don't let me oversleep. Okay?" He kissed her again, grabbed his belongings and trudged up the steps.

Katie went back to bed but sleep was elusive. Her mind was like a crowded racetrack. Mishaps were inevitable. The last time she remembered checking, it was five o'clock. The next sound she heard was Jeremy's beefed-up truck pulling into the driveway. Panic seized her as the clock declared it was after nine. She grabbed her robe and hurriedly opened the door.

Jeremy stared. "Why aren't you dressed ... and whose Ferrari is sitting in the driveway?"

"Shhh. Get in here and be quiet," she said as she yanked him inside.

Jeremy did a detective three-sixty scan of the place and whispered. "What is going on, Katie?"

Before she could answer, JD barreled into the room and leaped into Jeremy's arms. "Daddy!"

"You aren't dressed either. Exactly what went on after I left last night? And whose hot toy is in the driveway?"

Katie's surprise visitor stepped into view sporting messed-up hair, bare feet and an untucked shirt. "That would be mine. Name is Kyle Butler. Katie's fiancé." He offered his right hand. "You must be the other daddy."

Jeremy glanced at Katie's nightclothes and studied Kyle for an uncomfortable moment before responding. "Name is Jeremiah Webster. As far as I know I'm JD's only dad at the moment." His eyes locked with Kyle's as his son watched the exchange.

The atmosphere thickened quickly. Katie's anger-filled eyes focused on Jeremy.

Sensing her exasperation, he offered a compromise. "What if I take care of JD during the visitation and funeral? That will give you two the day together."

She softened. "Thanks. Would you mind getting him dressed? Kyle showed up unexpectedly, and it seems we all overslept."

In spite of his best efforts, the fog thickened and turned a deeper shade of green. "And exactly what time was that?"

"Six hours ago. Not that it's any of your business ... Kyle has been resting upstairs ... alone."

While that statement seemed to appease Jeremy, it definitely ruffled the other man who put a possessive arm around Katie.

"Upstairs, huh?" Jeremy whisked JD to his room.

Katie breathed a sigh of relief and pulled away from Kyle ... only to find his blue eyes glistening with green highlights. "You'd better get ready, Kyle. We are running late."

"This conversation is not over." He bristled and stormed back up the stairs. Katie hurried to her suite to heed her own advice.

Thirty minutes later, Jeremy tapped on her door. "We are out of here. I'll pick up JD's breakfast on the way." She breathed a sigh of relief when she heard the Webster males exited the house.

As she finished her hair and searched for a necklace, Kyle moved into her doorway. "I don't like that man being around you ... period."

"Kyle, he is JD's father. What did you expect?"

"I'm not sure, but certainly not *Ebony's* cover model cozying up to my wife-to-be." He moved into her suite to fasten her necklace. "How's the town responding to JD?"

"Pretty normal, I guess. Having Jeremy around helps."

"You still care for him?" Kyle asked as he perched on a nearby chair.

As she replayed the tone of those words, she couldn't decide if he was asking a question or making a statement. She glanced at him in the mirror. "I won't lie to you. Seeing him has stirred memories and resurrected old feelings ... for both of us. He's asking for a second chance."

The man leaped out of his chair like a boxer coming out of his corner for the next round. "Wait a minute. I thought he was engaged."

She twisted her ring. "He is ... but plans to break it off tonight."

Anger surfaced. "Do you have the same plans?"

Katie rotated to face him. "Does it mean nothing to you that I'm still wearing your ring?"

He sank back in his chair. "Visions of you and Jeremy together have tormented me. That's why I showed up this morning. I wanted to be sure there wasn't any hanky-panky going on." He reached for her left hand. "You haven't had this ring on three days, and I'm afraid you're going to give it back."

She moved close. "Kyle, today I have to bury my mother. Can we talk about us later?"

He pulled her onto his lap. "Forgive me, Katie. Tell me what I need to do."

"Keep Aunt Edith away. That will be difficult since she can smell money a mile away, and you reek of it. Think I can handle everyone else."

He hugged her. "Today I'll be your knight-in-shining-armor."

She finger combed his sandy blonde hair. "No, today we announce our engagement."

"Don't take this the wrong way, Sweetheart, but I'm glad your folks shipped you off to Roanoke."

"Life is crazy, isn't it? Aunt Bea would say that is God bringing good things out of our bad situations."

"I'm not a God fan, but I hope I'm the good that came out of Roanoke." Kyle was studying the house and its contents. "Did your mom leave you any of this?"

"Surprisingly, all of it." The grandfather clock in the foyer chimed ten times. "We need to get a move on."

Kyle proved himself exemplary that day. Introducing him as her fiancé instilled surprising confidence and pride. By the end of the burial, he was her hero. "I wish you didn't have to leave."

"Work beckons. Besides only extreme fatigue enabled me to sleep under the same roof and stay out of your room. I'm going home because I love you, Katie."

As she watched him drive away, Aunt Edith joined her. "Katie Williams, I can't believe you are engaged to such a remarkable, young man. Your parents would be proud of you."

"I didn't choose him because he's wealthy or white, Aunt Edith. I chose him because he loves my biracial son whom you and my parents wanted me to kill or abandoned."

Instead of her usual prudish facial contortions, Edith simulated an appeasing expression. "Now, Katie. You need to be more forgiving."

Hypocrite! Katie turned towards the Webster men. "Think I'll join my son and his father now, if you don't mind." She walked away with anger and pity dueling it out.

JD was asleep on Jeremy's shoulder. "How did it go, Katie?"

"Except for Aunt Edith, better than I expected … thanks to you and Kyle. I am weary and drained. Mind taking us home before she attacks again?"

"Sure thing." Jeremy walked to his vehicle, buckled JD into his seat and opened the door for Katie. "I need to find out whose car is blocking the exit."

By the time he got back to his truck, both his passengers were asleep. As he drove them home, he reflected on the day. Although he and JD stayed away from Kyle and Katie, he kept them in his sights. He could no longer deny that she cared for the man, but even more obvious was the fact that Kyle adored Katie.

He retrieved the house key in the courtyard—that had to change—and opened the door. After getting JD settled in his bed, he returned for Katie. She stirred as he lifted her into his arms. "Hold on, Sweetheart."

Half asleep, she wrapped her arms around his neck and rested her head on his shoulders. He lowered her onto the sofa. "Rest. I'll stick around until the buddy wakes up." He placed a throw over her and quietly crept into JD's room. Reclining next to his son, he fell asleep with images of Katie and Kyle tumbling around inside his head.

Five

A ringing phone woke everyone at the same time. Jeremy made a mad dash for the one in the hall and heard Kyle's voice. "Just wanted you to know I made it home safely."

Sleepy laughter filled the airwaves. "Would you believe we've slept the entire time you've been driving? Promise you'll get some decent sleep tonight, Kyle."

"Will do. Love you, Katie."

"Love you too, Kyle."

Jeremy waited until he heard two clicks, and then hung up. *She is going to walk out of my life again.*

JD was now wide-awake and announcing his need of food. "Come on, Pal. Let's go see what we can find."

As the men folks marched into the kitchen, Katie joined them. "Can you believe we slept that long?"

"Considering the night you had? Yes. But right now our son isn't concerned with the clock. His tummy is making strange noises. Right, Buddy?" JD was nodding while stuffing a deviled egg in his mouth.

"Let's see what else we can find in this over-filled refrigerator,"

Jeremy said as he placed a tray of sandwiches and a bowl of potato salad on the counter.

Katie answered the ringing phone. Her expression sobered immediately. "Yes, he is. Just a moment, please." A look of compassion washed over her. "Guess who."

Jeremy kept his eyes on Katie while listening to the other woman in his life. "Yes, I understand, Valerie. No, you cannot come here."

He reached for a ham and cheese sandwich. "Yes. Katie is white." He held the receiver away from his ear until the chatter on the other end subsided. "Yes, we have a son." Again, the receiver was distanced from his ear. "Yes, I've been spending as much time with him as possible." A smile emerged. "Yes, his mother has been present most of the time." Silence. "You have every right to be upset, Valerie. I do owe you an explanation. I'll be there in twenty minutes."

After hanging up, he stuffed a sandwich and apple in a bag. "The rumor mill hit the ER today. Upset just got redefined."

"You've embarrassed and hurt her, Jeremy. Shame on you."

He grabbed a drink, reminded JD to take care of his mama, and then asked Katie to walk him to the door.

"I don't want to hurt Valerie, Katie, but I love you."

"Hmmm. Are you going to tell *Miss Valentine* that?"

He stepped close. "I am."

Katie's demeanor softened. "She won't appreciate your truthfulness right now, but I think your silence would hurt more. Please let her know that I still intend to marry Kyle."

"I won't leave anything out. The pain I may cause her is nothing compared to what I did to you and JD. I hope she can see that."

Tears threatened to escape. "I wouldn't count on that if I were you."

He saluted and left with less than his usual Marine confidence regarding this *disengagement*.

Six

Katie spent the next day dealing with her mom's estate. A conversation with Isaac and an appointment with her mom's attorney pointed her in the right direction. After filing the will with the probate court, she tackled the task of dealing with Martha's personal belongings.

To her chagrin, Katie discovered she couldn't sort out or pack up the remnants of her Asheville life as easily or neatly as her mom's. Truth? Coming back home had complicated her and JD's lives. To be more specific … Jeremy Webster had thrown a monkey wrench into her plans.

By the end of the day, she had come to two conclusions. She had to get away from him to think clearly and she needed some time with Aunt Bea. That translated into a return to Roanoke. Circling October 14 solidified her decision. Kyle would be elated. Jeremy and JD? Probably not.

The camaraderie that continued to develop between father and son the next few days was not only heart-warming, but guilt producing. She had robbed them of each other, and now she was going to separate them again.

"You okay, Katie?" Jeremy inquired one evening.

She lied and nodded as two tears escaped.

His forehead wrinkled. "Are those happy or sad tears?"

"One of each I think "

He turned to JD. "Mama needs a hug. Wanna help me?"

JD climbed onto the sofa and snuggled in her lap. Jeremy approached from the back. His cheek was snug against hers. His breath smelled like sweet mint. His cologne was familiar. Old memories stirred. Her body and heart reacted.

With a practiced coolness, she asked, "Did you and Valerie come to an understanding?"

He straightened and moved to the spot beside her. "We'll talk about that later. My folks have invited you and JD to supper tonight. How about it?"

Remembering how awkward she felt around them at the funeral ruled that out. "You're welcome to take JD, Jeremy, but I'm won't be going." Checking JD's clothes for stains or dirt, she asked, "Does he look okay?"

"Son, will you go make a monster for Grammy and Papa? Daddy needs to talk with Mama."

Thick, long eyelashes shaded his green, entreating eyes. "Mama, I have a papa and a grammy now. Can't we please go?"

"Yeah and they're more excited than you are, Son," Jeremy chimed in as he and JD headed for his play dough tubs. "I'll help you put down the plastic cloth."

A few minutes later Jeremy found Katie in the kitchen emptying the dishwasher. "Sweetheart, my folks want to apologize. I wish you'd reconsider."

"I appreciate the thought, but I'm still engaged." Caring eyes met his. "How is Valerie?"

His countenance changed. "Furious. Hurt. It's been rough, but I think she has finally accepted the fact that it's over … even if *you* walk away from *me* this time."

"And what part of that surprised you?" She moved to the fireplace and threw another log on the fire. "Rejection hurts, Jeremy."

"True, but rejection because of a white woman makes it harder for Valerie. I saw first-hand the subtle ways our history still plays into our present. There were moments it felt like I was forsaking my own to embrace an enemy."

"Me? An enemy?"

"In her mind you represent those who have been and some who continue to be. I walked away from her with an acute awareness that the love you and I share is a rare gift. God has enabled us to see the beauty in our differences and that has forged a love that bridges the abyss that prejudice and ignorance had hollowed out over the years."

He helped with the dishes. "Valerie threatened to confront you. Hopefully I nipped that in the bud."

"I wouldn't turn her away, although I'm not sure what I'd say." When all dishes were in place, Katie hung up the drying cloth. "You two go on."

"The folks will be disappointed." Melancholy and frustration took over his expression as he stared into the fire.

Their son entered with two new monster creations and a question. "Daddy, do you love my mama?"

Jeremy's face lit up. "With all my heart and I have five years to make up for." He proceeded to pepper JD with kisses. "And I love you bunches and have four years to make up for."

When Jeremy backed off for fear his son might have an accident, JD began covering his dad's face with sloppy kisses. "I love you bunches too, Dad."

JD halted abruptly and turned to Katie. "Mama, do you love my daddy?"

Katie had been refusing to answer that question since the moment he showed up on her doorstep. She shook her head but the waterworks that followed contradicted her response.

Jeremy had JD snug in his arms. "I think Mama needs some of your kisses, Son."

When JD leaned in to kiss Katie, Jeremy whispered. "We have the makings of a remarkable family here, Lady." He kissed her on the cheek, and he and JD left without another word.

Katie called Aunt Bea and then Kyle. All during the calls, she had to reel in her thoughts that kept drifting to the Webster men.

One hour later, Jeremy returned … minus her son. "Where is JD?" she asked without inviting him in.

"Having a blast getting to know his grandparents."

She backed away as if he were an intruder. "Jeremy Webster, you have no right …"

He interrupted. "No right? What kind of right did you have to keep him from me those four years, Katie? I am asking for one night with him and some time with you. Is that too much to ask after five years of secrets and silence?"

She wrapped her arms around her trembling body.

"Look, Katie, I'll go get him if you insist, but will you give me one hour … just us."

Didn't he understand? It was the *just us* that petrified her. "What do we have to talk about?"

"Katie, may I come in?"

Zombie-like she moved away from the door and led the way into the hearth room. She watched Jeremy feed the fire and refilled the log tray from the outside ricks. When he settled in a nearby chair, his green eyes focused on her.

"Jeremy, it's too late for us."

"I won't settle for visitation rights, Katie. I'll seek joint custody."

She rose from the sofa and faced the fire. "I won't fight you."

He moved to her side. "I checked out your Roanoke boyfriend. I guess you know that you're hobnobbing with the crème de la crème, Katie. His folks are part of the higher echelon of society. Vanderbilt-type folks. How did the two of you get hooked up anyway?"

Katie's head jerked around. "Are you sure about that?"

"Oh, Honey, I had the entire department drooling by the time I finished researching the Roanoke Butlers. Have you checked out Forbes lately? How can you be engaged to the man and not know?"

Katie lifted her hand. "I accepted this ring six hours before arriving here. Up until then, I had tried to keep our relationship on a work and friendship basis. It was the love that grew between him and JD that swayed me." She looked up. "I knew they weren't poor, but I never dreamed they were *that* kind of rich."

Jeremy grabbed her shoulders. "Katie, JD has a father. You can marry for love now."

She brushed off his hands. "Just because he's rich doesn't mean he doesn't have feelings, Jeremy. I can't do to him what you did to Valerie. Besides, I do love him … in my own way."

Jeremy wondered aimlessly around the room. "Most of those folks marry within their own ranks. I'm wondering if the man truly loves you or finds you challenging because you aren't impressed with his bank accounts."

He stopped in front of her. "His pedigree and assets make me feel like a poor country mouse. He can offer you the world and probably throw in a galaxy or two. I can offer you love and guarantee you a world of prejudice bigger than the one you've already entered … plus the uncertainties of a husband in law enforcement."

Katie was pondering the enlightening information regarding Kyle and his family when she vaguely heard Jeremy say something about moving in with his parents.

"Why would you do that?"

"I will need their help with JD."

"You don't share custody of our child yet, Jeremy."

"No, but I'm making plans. You're returning to Roanoke, aren't you?"

When she started to answer, he put a finger on her lips and then seized a hand. "Shhh! Please listen. Katie, I lost you once and losing you again has me so unsettled that I'm driving my partner crazy. But to take JD away is asking too much."

"How did you know?" She attempted to free her hand, but found it interlaced with his.

His other hand cradled her chin. "It's in your eyes and stilted conversations. This time it's you who are walking … no, you're running away, because you are afraid of what will happen if you stay."

She couldn't hold his gaze. He had read her mind and she had no rebuttal.

He kissed every finger before releasing her hand. "This is the part I've wrestled with the most. I know you still have feelings for me, but I also know you care for Kyle. So who owns your heart, Katie? Your old love or your new? In your search for the answer, in fairness to all of us, will you give me the same chance you've given Kyle?"

She moved to the closest phone and held it in his direction. "Call your folks and let me talk to JD."

What was she up to? "Yeah, let me talk to my little buddy, Dad."

Katie reached for the receiver. "JD, your daddy wants you to spend the night with him and your grandparents. I'll bet he would let you sleep with him," she said as her eyes took in Jeremy's stunned expression.

"Tell him yes," he whispered.

"Daddy said yes, JD."

"Ask him if you can stay, too, Mama? I don't want you to get lonesome."

"Mama will be okay, JD. You be good for Grammy and Papa until Daddy gets home, okay?"

"Gotta go now, Mama. My horsey is waiting."

"I love you." She was almost in tears.

"You're not going to cry, are you, Mama?"

She sobered up. "No, JD, I'm not going to cry."

She hung up and crumbled. "I lied."

He kissed the top of her head. "Katie, if you marry Kyle, you and JD will spend lots of nights apart."

She moved out of his range of touch. "I think that's one of the reasons for this crying spell. This is our first night apart."

He reached for his jacket. "Care to share what else might be involved?"

"My heart that roams between here and Roanoke … between you and Kyle. I left Roanoke ready to marry him. I will leave Asheville aware of my resurrected feelings for you. I cannot hurt him, Jeremy."

They walked to the door together. "If love is not enough, Katie,

I'll lose, because it's all I have to offer. That and our son." He kissed her on the cheek.

"Some folks would say that's a loaded hand, Mr. Webster."

"Guess that depends on what the other man has been dealt. If that's the case, I don't have a prayer."

"Goodnight, Jeremy."

"Night, Katie."

Seven

The sleepover encouraged JD to stay with his daddy and grandparents when Katie returned to Roanoke. Kyle was not pleased about that development, but he was thrilled his girl was returning.

Katie arrived at her apartment Sunday afternoon and before she could get her luggage out of the car, Kyle pulled in her driveway in a new Mercedes Benz Roadster. "Let me help you with those." He leaned close and kissed her cheek.

"Your timing is perfect." Glancing at his choice of vehicle, she added, "New toy? Aunt Edith would lick your boots to be seen in that vehicle."

Once they had her luggage inside, she helped him retrieve groceries from his car. "I'm not trying to impress your stuffy aunt, Katie. How do *you* like it?"

She rubbed her hands along the sleek lines. "Kyle, any car with more paint and fewer dents than my ancient Camaro is attractive."

He smiled and followed her inside. "Thought I'd make supper tonight."

Katie eyed the man. "You can cook?"

"I have a few secrets tucked away, Katie."

That reminded her of Jeremy's revelation. "Kyle, why do you want to marry me?"

Laying aside the food, he faced her. "Because I love you is not going to be enough, is it? What's going on?"

Katie glanced at the ring. "I learned some interesting facts about you and your family while in Asheville."

He reached for her hand. "Let me guess. Detective Webster."

Her gaze was riveted on this mysterious man whose ring she wore. "You are avoiding my question."

His eyes took on a faraway look. "None of us get to choose our parents or the circumstances of our birth, Katie, but as adults we can choose to stay locked within our narrow and limited world or we can explore the other worlds around us. Before you, I never wanted to explore outside my world. Meeting you changed my mind."

His focus shifted to her. "Katie, the student, intrigued me with her creative and out of the box ideas. Katie, the woman, attracted me with her beauty and character. Katie, the mother, stirred a longing for my own family. Katie, the champion of the underdogs of life, was my undoing. I purposely kept you out of my world, because I love who you are in yours. Are you upset with me?"

"No, just surprised and questioning if I belong in your fairy tale."

"Trust me, Cinderella; you bring rare gifts to my needy world."

Katie took careful measure of this man. He was at least three inches taller and probably thirty pounds heavier than Jeremy. Deep-set, sky blue eyes, sandy blonde hair and the rugged good looks of his dad made him a very attractive man's man. How many other secrets was he holding close?

She studied the ring again, then reached for the phone. "Let me check in with JD, and then we'll see what kind of chef you really are."

The Webster boys were out for a burger according to Grammy Webster who promised to deliver her message. When she hung up, she caught Kyle leaning against the kitchen counter studying her.

"You look like JD when he's been up to mischief."

"Is your little interrogation over?" A mischievous smile stretched from ear to ear. "More importantly, did I pass?"

"For now." Katie retrieved a cold ginger ale.

Kyle pushed off the counter and returned to his tasks. "Are you aware how little time you and I have had alone? I need to thank Jeremy for setting this up."

He had the sauce cooking, the noodles boiled and the meat browning while Katie assembled the salad. After wiping his hands on a towel, he rounded the bar. Leaning down, he nibbled on an ear and moved to her lips. "I've missed you."

She flushed and put a hand on his chest. "I haven't been gone that long, Mr. Butler."

"First time you've been gone since we met. What did Professor Higgins say about his *Fair Lady*? 'I've grown accustomed to her face.'" He half-sung, half-spoke several more lines. "Truth is I can't imagine life without you, and I intend to do whatever it takes to make sure I never have to find out what that would be like."

She downed half of the ginger ale trying to drown her resurrected feelings for Jeremy Webster.

After placing the tray of lasagna in the oven, he removed the apron and faced her. "Have you thought about where we'll live, Katie?"

"No, and I wouldn't know where to start looking."

"Then I have a marvelous suggestion."

Catching the gleam in his eyes gave birth to a thought so farfetched it scared her spitless. Her heart rate doubled.

"Penny for your thoughts," he said nonchalantly.

"Surely you didn't ..." She could not finish the sentence. She downed the rest of the ginger ale hoping it would calm the escalating turbulence in her gut.

"While the lasagna is in the oven, let's take a ride." Without further discussion, he snatched her jacket and wrapped it around her shoulders. "Let's go."

Katie was so nervous she could swear Noah was using her body to gather the animals.

The new car purred out of the driveway, turned north and headed into the old historic residential section. Twenty minutes later, Katie realized the reality exceeded her imagination when he turned into the driveway of the house of her dreams.

"Kyle?" she finally managed in a panicked voice. He hurried to her side and helped her out.

"How did you manage to get hold of this place?"

"This has been in the works for some time now."

Before they made it to the door, an elderly couple exited the house across the street and made a beeline for the two Ks. "Are you the couple who bought this place?" They introduced themselves as the Burns.

With his right hand extended and the other nestled around Katie's waist, Kyle introduced himself and added, "This is my wedding gift for Katie."

Knowing her ability to litter folks with the contents of her nerves, Katie quickly excused herself and dashed to a more private spot in the back lawn. After fertilizing one of the big trees, she heard Mrs. Burns' shrill voice. "Oh, but you do plan to marry before moving in, don't you?" Katie held her breath waiting for Kyle's answer. Nothing. Had the man passed out or was he searching for her?

Hoping the ark and its animals had cleared out, Katie rushed to the front to find Kyle and Mr. Burns discussing the stock market plunge of the day. The hand wringing, distraught female repeated her ignored question to Katie.

"Mrs. Burns, if we move in … I promise you we will be married."

Kyle abruptly excused himself and handed Katie the key. "Would you mind opening the door to the house with your name on the deed and then explain *if* to the man whose ring is on your finger?"

Her dream house had her name on the deed? She didn't have to look around. She had studied every nook and cranny of this house as part of her apprentice assignment that dealt with updating old treasures while preserving their history. "Your extravagance overwhelms me, Kyle." She yielded to the urge to hug him. "You know I love this place."

"That's better." Leading her through the house rich with evidence of their combined talents, Kyle asked, "So Katie, if you love me … and this place … what's the problem?"

Unable to verbalize her own reservations released another disturbance in her digestive system. "You'll have to excuse me, Kyle. I'm still queasy." After gagging until she couldn't, she rested on a fainting couch for a few minutes before exiting. Kyle was leaning against the wall. "What's going on, Katie?"

"Have you forgotten I know what this property is worth? I've lived in a cracker box for five years and survived on peanut butter and jelly sandwiches more days than I care to think about. You are overwhelming me, Kyle."

He reached for her hand and led her to the sofa in the formal living room. "Is it just the money, Katie?"

She slipped her hand from his and took in the elegant room. "When we worked on this house, I was a struggling student and this was a senior project. I was comfortable with that, but to call it home? I don't know if I can." She stared at the ring. "And no … it's not just the money."

He knelt in front of her. "Then help me understand."

She studied the man who had wormed his way into her heart by loving her son. "Kyle, I've seriously considered returning this ring and telling you and Jeremy both that JD and I will be fine on our own."

The man's countenance fell. "Please don't do that, Katie."

She put a finger on his lips. "Jeremy helped me understand my dilemma. I am torn between the man of my past and the man of my present. I have to find out who owns my heart."

Kyle's blue eyes lit up. "He suggested that?"

"He did."

Kyle jumped to his feet and pulled her to hers. "This house is my attempt to please you. If it doesn't, I'll sell it."

Katie slowly shook her head. "You intrigue me, Kyle Butler. Rich, but not snobbish. Spoiled but not obnoxious. Determined, but not unyielding. Over the top at times, but willing to concede."

"Only with you, Katie, only with you." He handed her the house key. "Lock up. We have supper in the oven." As they neared the vehicle, he handed her a different set of keys. "Check out the new wheels."

Driving his new car was another taste of his world. "Sweet machine," she said as they turned into Aunt Bea's driveway.

"I'm glad you like it." He opened the glove compartment. "Your name is on the title."

First the house and now the car. "Kyle, you have to stop this."

"What? Making sure you have a decent car I can trust when you're on the road?" He folded the title and placed it in her purse. "Can't help it, Katie. I've waited a long time to pamper the woman of my dreams. You'll just have to tolerate my folly for a while."

He was right. She needed a paradigm shift if she was going to marry this man. "Will you keep it at your place until we marry? Mom's car is a definite improvement over my old one."

"At least you're not refusing it."

The aroma of Italian cuisine filled the little space as they entered. "If it's half as delicious as it smells, you may need to change your profession, Mr. Butler."

"You jest, Katie, but if I thought it would help me win your heart, I'd do it."

Katie pondered that statement, but made no comment. As they were eating, she broached a subject Jeremy had brought up. "Kyle, I feel like I know your dad fairly well in the work environment, but I'd like to spend some time getting to know your parents on a personal level."

"That can be arranged."

"How much have you told them about me? About JD?"

He finished the bite in his mouth and pushed back from the table. "Everything, but only after you accepted my ring."

"How did they respond?"

"Let's just say they're not willing to risk losing their only son. I'll arrange for us to spend time with them while you're here."

The rest of their evening together was pleasant. "I have Saturday tickets to the playhouse. *Phantom of the Opera* is playing. Interested?"

"Definitely."

After cleaning the kitchen and playing a couple of games of scrabble, they called it a night … after Katie convinced him the boundaries had not changed.

The next morning she called the Websters to check on JD. "Is that you, Mama?"

"Yeah, it's me." Hearing his voice made her want to pack and leave now.

"Can I come live with you? I don't like you so far away?" She heard sniffles.

"Oh, JD, Mama should have brought you with her."

"Daddy misses you too, Mama."

Another voice joined the conversation. "Either you come get him or I can bring him to you. My next day off is three days away."

She looked at the clock. "JD, it will take Mama five or six hours to get there."

"Promise you'll be here tonight, Mama?"

"Lord willing, Son, I'll be there." A phone clicked. "Did he just hang up on me?"

"He's happy again. Please be careful and let me know when you arrive. Okay?"

"You worry too much, Sergeant." Images of him in his uniform filled her head.

"Well, it just so happens that I'm crazy about this little man that bears my likeness, and I'm concerned about his mama spending time with another man. Guess I do have a sizable case of worries right now."

"See you later, Jeremy."

She hung up and called Kyle. "I've got to make an emergency trip home to pick up JD."

"I'd drive you down, but I have meetings I can't miss. Would you consider driving the Roadster?"

"Mom's car is fine, Kyle. Thanks for the offer."

"I love you, Katie."

She hesitated. "And I love you."

One hour later, she was on the road back to Asheville.

Eight

Katie pulled into the Webster's driveway by mid-afternoon. A knock brought her son and his grandmother to the door. JD leaped into her arms. "Mama, can I come live with you again?"

"That's why I'm here." Showers of kisses turned his giggles into rumbles of laughter. "Daddy kisses me like that too, Mama."

When JD's excitement leveled off, Jeannie interjected, "Have you made contact with Jeremy since you arrived?"

"No, I figured he'd stop by this evening to see JD."

"Oh, heavens to Betsy, Child. That man has developed a bad case of nerves. It wouldn't surprise me if he has the hives. Please call and relieve him of his misery."

Kind eyes peered into Katie's soul. "Doc and I were wrong, Honey. I hope you can find it in your heart to forgive us."

Katie wasn't ready for that yet. If it wasn't for this woman and her husband, she and Jeremy would have married five years ago. "Thanks for taking care of JD." Turning to her son, she asked, "Are your clothes together?"

"Yes, Ma'am. Grammy helped me pack everything in a new traveling bag Daddy bought me."

All the way to Wimberley Estates, JD yakked about his new daddy and grandparents. "Why didn't we find them sooner, Mama?"

Jeannie's apology and JD's delight and question drove a wedge into her root of bitterness. "Someday I'll tell you our story, but right now all you need to know is your mama and daddy love you."

After JD settled, she dialed Jeremy's work number. "Webster here."

"Jeremy, I made the trip safely."

"How long are you staying?"

She could hear the trepidation in his voice. "Until Saturday morning."

Dead silence followed.

"Kyle will be a good husband and make JD a great number two daddy, Jeremy."

The airwaves were silent so long she wondered if he had hung up ... still she waited.

"May I come over after work?"

"JD will be upset if you don't."

"What about you?"

"See you at six o'clock, Jeremy." She hung up.

After digging out a pork chop and rice recipe, she headed to the grocery. When she was not with JD or going through more of her mom's stuff, she was busy preparing one of Jeremy's favorite meals. Why? She wasn't sure. Maybe to ease her conscience.

The man's middle name could have been *Dependable*. Six o'clock the door chimes were ringing. "Unlock the door for your daddy, Son."

When JD persuaded Jeremy to watch a *Veggie Tales* video, Katie escaped to the kitchen to finish supper. Lost in her thoughts, she was unaware that the object of her deliberations had entered the kitchen area ... alone. "Katie, why are you unwilling to give me another chance?"

She jerked around and stumbled as her feet tangled with his. Jeremy's hands on her shoulders brought out her defenses. "Your window of opportunity closed five years ago."

"Katie, was my wrong choice any worse than yours?" He backed away but his eyes sustained contact. "I thought you were working on forgiveness."

"What do you suggest I do, Jeremy? What do I tell Kyle?"

His green lasers were penetrating her defenses. "The truth. That you and I need some time together … without his ring between us. If in the end you choose him, I'll concede."

JD walked in. "Mama, can Daddy spend the night with us? I want both of you at the same time."

Jeremy deflected her accusing glare with his innocent face and open hands. "I had no part in that statement, but I second the motion. Can you honestly tell me you've not thought about it?"

When Katie turned away without answering, Jeremy slumped in the closest chair.

"Daddy, why are you sad?"

"Because I don't want to lose you and Mama again, JD."

The boy crawled in his dad's lap and wrapped strong little arms around his neck. "Don't worry, Daddy. We're never going to lose you again."

Katie directed her attention to finishing the broccoli salad. To her surprise Jeremy reached for her left hand, removed the ring and kissed her until desire consumed her body and her resistance melted.

"Now, Lady, I hope you are as confused and tormented as I am." Without another word, he stormed out of the house.

When Katie slid the ring back on her finger, she sensed the distance it put between them.

JD had watched with interest. "Mama, where did Daddy go?"

"Daddy has lots of things on his mind, JD. You and I need to eat. He'll be back."

Jeremy didn't return until JD was getting out of the bathtub. When he walked in, Katie walked out.

"Daddy, where you did go? Mama cried again."

"She did?"

"Uh-huh."

Jeremy apologized as he helped JD with his pajamas and teeth before carrying him to his bedroom. "I want Mama to come too, Daddy."

"I'll get her." He found Katie sitting in front of the fireplace … staring into flames. "JD is asking for you."

Without a look or comment, she complied. JD handed the storybook to Jeremy. "Read to me, Daddy."

The boy was asleep before the story was over. After they exited his room, Jeremy reached for her hand and walked to the front door. "Forgive me for my behavior, Katie. From this moment on, I'll make every effort to respect your engagement to Kyle and deal with my loss."

She withdrew her hand and looked at Kyle's ring. "I'm confused, Jeremy."

"Me too, Katie." He walked away … but his words and kiss lingered.

Sleep abandoned her that night. Her tangled covers mirrored her thoughts. In desperation, she blurted it all out … in case God was interested or listening.

With the newspaper and a fresh cup of coffee in her hands the next morning, Katie read the headlines, checked out the sports section, then turned to the human-interest section. Her favorite advice column's heading gently tugged at her heart. *To Err is Human. To Forgive is Divine.* Seeing unforgiveness in someone else's life helped put hers in perspective. Could she forgive Jeremy and his parents? They had forgiven her.

By noon, she left word for Jeremy to stop by at seven p.m. At four o'clock, she called Roanoke. "It's Katie, Kyle."

"Hi, Sweetheart. How are my two favorite people doing?"

Unease swept over her as she anticipated his response to her proposal. "JD is having adjustment problems. His attachment to Jeremy continues to grow. He wants his dad to spend the nights so his mom and dad are together … with him."

The sound of heavy breathing and a chair creaking echoed through the lines. She could visualize his facial responses. "I hope you explained that is impossible under the circumstances."

"Of course I did."

Other sounds filtering through the lines indicated more movement. "That man is still in love with you, Katie."

"He readily admits that, Kyle. He has asked for the same chance at a relationship that I've given you."

That sounded like a moving desk. A sternness was now evident in his tone. "He had his chance and blew it. Remember? You're wearing my ring and I'm asking both of you to respect that fact."

"Trust me. Your ring plays a huge part in controlling his behavior."

"I'm surprised, but pleased to hear that. Are you still planning to be back by Saturday?"

"Yes." Digging deep for the courage she needed, Katie offered her thoughts. "Kyle, I'm considering Jeremy's suggestion. You and I have been together for over a year. Jeremy and I have spent fragments of fourteen days together in the last five years."

"And whose fault is that?"

She could hear the anger building. "Actually his and mine." Something fell or crashed on his end of the line. "Are you okay?"

A few bad words slipped out. "I'm a lot of things right now, but okay is not one of them. So what is the real purpose of this conversation, Katie?"

"I won't be wearing your ring for a while."

Visualizing his response was not hard after working with him the last twelve months. A strained, but controlled voice responded. "I'm going to hang up before I say something I'll regret. Promise I'll see you Saturday?"

"Promise. Thank you, Kyle."

He laughed sarcastically. "For what?"

The line went quiet, but not her heart. After cradling the receiver, she removed Kyle's ring and secured it in the safe. Interesting how something so small can say so much.

The doorbell rang in the middle of JD's bath that evening. "That will be your daddy. I'll let him in." She flipped on the outside lights and unlocked the door.

"I suggest you leave those outside lights on all night, every night, Katie," he said as he moved into the foyer.

"Good evening to you, too, Sergeant. Have you eaten?"

Yeah, Maw fed me. Where's my boy?"

When Katie pointed towards his bathroom. Jeremy hung his coat in the closet and headed down the hall. She went to the kitchen to make some hot cider. To help quieten her increasing case of nerves, she grabbed a book and a ginger ale before settling in front of the fire.

It wasn't long before Jeremy entered with JD on his shoulders. "Look at me, Mama. I'm the Jolly Green Giant. Ho, ho, ho."

"And what do you grow in your gardens, Mr. Jolly Giant?"

He put his hands on Jeremy's head and leaned close. "What are we growing, Daddy?"

Jeremy whispered.

With a gruff voice the kid announced, "*Snips and snails and puppy-dog tails.*"

She pointed to the decanter of hot cider. "Well, I'm out of those yummy snacks, but I do have some hot cider and almond biscotti."

JD's eyes got big. "Let me down, Daddy. I love those biscuits."

Katie watched the giant dismantle and partake of the treat. As she cradled her own cup of hot cider, Jeremy did a double take when he noticed the missing ring. "Wh-what happened?"

"We'll talk after we put JD to bed."

As they tucked their tired, happy son in bed, his smile and words melted their hearts. "I like having a mama … and daddy."

When Katie leaned down to kiss him, he asked, "Mama, will you sing about the angels watching over me?"

She scooted close and sang the lullaby that has calmed his heart many nights. When she finished, JD pointed to Jeremy. "Will you pray with me, Daddy?"

Jeremy knelt by the lad and together they repeated *Now I lay me down to sleep* … with JD's additional thanks thrown in.

As they turned off his lights and walked out, Jeremy reached for Katie's left hand. "Tell me."

Katie led the way to the hearth room and shared the last

twenty-four hours … including her conversation with Kyle. Jeremy studied her intensely for a moment. "I feel like a silly school boy with his first crush. How do we start over, Katie, when my heart is so deeply involved already? How is this going to work?"

Springing to her feet and heading towards the credenza, she pulled out a box. "Let's play a game or two of Yahtzee. You tell me about your time with the Marines, and I'll tell you about my years in Roanoke. We have some catching up to do."

"Good idea." The more they played and talked, the more it felt like old times. When the clock struck ten, Jeremy stood. "I need to get home. Tired deputies make reckless mistakes." He reached for her hands. "Thanks for tonight, Katie."

Awkwardness joined them as they walked to the door. Jeremy retrieved his jacket but lingered. "Is a kiss allowed?"

The man had appealed to her like no other since the night they met seven years ago. She glanced at her naked ring finger and nodded.

Gently cupping her face with his hands, Jeremy slowly and gently kissed her cheeks, her eyes, the tip of her nose and then her lips. "I've never loved anyone like I love you, Katie." He slipped off his jacket. "Leave the lights on and lock up." He stepped outside and drove off into the night.

For the first time since returning to Asheville, Katie had allowed herself to respond to the man and her renegade heart was defecting. What was she going to do?

The next time they were together, she set up a physical boundary. "No more kissing, Jeremy. I can't deny the chemistry is still between us, but that's where we messed up before. This time it has to be more."

"Are you going to hold Kyle to the same guidelines?"

"I don't know. The chemistry between us is not that strong."

Jeremy laughed. "Honey, I've got news for you. It may not be for you, but trust me, there is no shortage on his part."

Katie blushed. "Well, let's just say I have more resistance where he is concerned."

"Or maybe you're wiser this time, Katie."

"Whatever the reason, Jeremy, our physical contact is limited to holding hands and brief hugs."

As a result, their time together became a gentle reconnecting and getting to know the person each had become. The bonus was experiencing what being a family could be.

Friday night Jeremy took them to the Asheville High School football game. Their seats were close to the spot where they met. He pointed to the section and the row. "That's when your daddy knew he wanted to spend the rest of his life with your mama, JD."

While JD was energized by the enthusiastic crowd, old memories revitalized a buried love for Katie.

Their stay was cut short because of their son, but the impact of the night lingered the rest of the week.

Jeremy's departing words haunted her. "If we don't make it this time, the fault won't lie at my door, Katie. You'll have to leave me. I want us as much as JD does."

Nine

Hoping for some time with Aunt Bea before meeting Kyle, Katie had not alerted him of her exact arrival time Saturday. As they turned into the shared driveway, JD's excitement grew. "Aunt Bea's home, Mama. Can I go see her?"

"Sure. I'll be there when I get the car unloaded."

The phone rang as she emptied the last bag. It was Kyle. "Katie, there has been a change of plans. Would you allow JD to spend the night with Aunt Bea?"

"The night? What do you have in mind?"

"I'll explain when I get there."

At least he was in a good mood. "Oooo ... kay."

Katie spent the next two hours trying to explain her quandary to Aunt Bea between JD's chatty times.

"To be honest, Katie, I was surprised to hear you accepted Kyle's ring. I knew he had become a good friend, but I've seen no evidence of a woman in love."

Katie watched JD play with the train set. "He's the only man in five years who reached out to my son as well as me. I love him for that, Aunt Bea. Besides, he makes me feel safe and protected."

The rocking chair stopped. "Tell me how Jeremy makes you feel."

"Like I'm riding a roller coaster in the middle of a fireworks extravaganza."

Aunt Bea's soft blue eyes studied Katie. "We are back to one of our old topics you keep ignoring. You need to find your way into the arms of a loving God before you get serious about either man. Your safety and security shouldn't rest in a man, but in a relationship with God."

Katie sat on the floor hugging her legs. "I don't understand all your religious and philosophical jabber sometimes, Aunt Bea."

"I'm not talking about religion, Katie. Think of the relationship between you and JD. God wants that kind of connection with you."

The two talked until the clock reminded Katie of her plans for tonight. JD was happy to stay with Aunt Bea. "The boy and I will be fine. Enjoy yourself."

As Katie showered and dressed, Aunt Bea's words kept echoing in her head and resonating in her heart. Was the drought of God's love in her life the underlying cause of her men problems?

Taking a deep breath, she opened the door to her Roanoke challenge. Mercy! She had never seen him looking so good!

"Do I have shaving cream on my face?" He rubbed his hand across both cheeks.

She blushed. "No, it's just that … well, you are quite handsome this evening, Mr. Butler."

His blue eyes sparkled. "Glad my lady approves." After sharing a warm hug, he handed her a fancy garment bag. "These are for you … for tonight."

Her dumbfounded stare prompted further explanation. "Everything you need is included. Aunt Bea gave me sizes … in case you're wondering."

Wondering? Her thoughts were so frozen she couldn't muster a question. She managed to get out one word. "Kyle …"

The pendulum movement of his pointer started again. "Humor me, Katie. Just go get dressed."

With an increasingly queasy stomach, she obeyed. Unzipping the bag revealed the most beautiful burgundy dress she had ever seen. The brand was one she had only read about. Thankfully, someone had removed the price tag.

After slithering out of the nicest dress she had owned up to this moment, she carefully slipped on one that probably cost more than a week's paycheck. Glancing in the mirror proved it was not only gorgeous, but was a definite plus for her as well. The zip-up compartments of the bag bulged. The first pocket contained an embellished jewelry box with a triple strand of pearls and matching earrings. A larger pouch yielded a matching pair of burgundy heels. When she reached for the pearl-embossed evening purse, a note fell out.

Dearest Katie,

You are right. All this is just stuff and things. I can live without them. I'm not sure I'll make it without you.

All my love and all my stuff are yours.

Kyle

Confident in her appearance, Katie exited the bedroom. Kyle's approval oozed. "You … look … sensational!" Reaching for a smaller garment bag he must have brought in while she was changing, he pulled out a fashionable, matching shawl.

"Kyle, this is too …"

"Indulge me, Katie." He slipped the wrap over her shoulders and squeezed in a hug. "Mom and Dad are treating us to the weekend at the *Hotel Roanoke*. I have the other outfits you'll need. You might want to grab some toiletries and undies."

Other outfits? He led her back to the bedroom. "Aunt Bea promised to take good care of JD."

With robotic movements, she picked up her overnight case and retrieved the items in the bathroom. "Kyle …" was all she got out again.

He laughed. "We have established the fact that you know my name. I take the overnight case indicates you are accepting the offer." He lifted her left hand to his lips. "I intend to prove to you this weekend that you belong in my world, and my ring belongs on this finger."

Her eyes were filled with questions. "I'm so confused, Kyle."

"I understand, but this weekend … it's just the two of us. Okay?"

"Okay."

When Katie had first arrived in the valley, the Hotel Roanoke was closed. After several years and millions of dollars of extensive renovations, the 1882, Tudor Revival hotel, reopened its doors April of this year. When her class on architectural styles toured the newly opened hotel in May, Katie never dreamed she would be sleeping under its deeply pitched roof or enjoying its opulent accommodations.

When Kyle turned onto Shenandoah Avenue and parked in front of the nostalgic piece of history, she found herself speechless for the second time this evening. Before she could wrap her mind around all that was happening, a young valet opened her door. As Kyle escorted her into the lobby, she realized he was not only introducing her to his family this weekend, but inviting her into his world.

The ambiance of the place, a romantic evening of live music and incredible food, hobnobbing with his folks and their friends and the undivided attention of a southern gentleman gave Katie a heady feeling. She couldn't deny it. His world was alluring and intoxicating.

After the others called it a night, Katie and Kyle spent time by the outdoor fireplace reliving their history together. It was late when they headed for their rooms. Kyle slipped her key in the lock and opened her door. "Thanks for one of the most amazing nights of my life, Kyle." Her heart was as flighty as her head. "I think my name could be Cinderella tonight."

He stepped into her room. "Unlike the fairy tale, the magic doesn't have to end, Katie."

What was he insinuating? "Kyle, we have had this discussion."

He moved to the sitting area and loosened his tie. "Not this one, Katie. Shut the door, please."

Stunned, she glanced between him and the door. "You can't stay."

"I suggest you close the door unless you want others to hear a very private conversation."

Slowly she closed the door and watched him remove his jacket and tie. "What are you doing?"

He smiled. "Getting comfortable." He patted the space beside him. "Come sit. We need to talk."

Her euphoric intoxication was neutralized by a dose of reality. "About?"

"Us, of course." He removed one shoe and then the other.

"I wish you'd stop undressing, Kyle."

He laughed. "Though my room is next door and I have the key that joins them, you can relax. I'm not going to take advantage of you."

"Then what is going on?" She gestured to his discarded attire.

He reached for her hand and pulled her beside him. "If I remember your proposal when you removed my ring, you said Jeremy wanted and needed the same chance at a relationship you had given me the last year. Is that correct?"

"Something like that."

"And have you and he been spending time together since then?" His eyes were probing.

"Yes." Before she could tell him about the boundaries that were in place, he continued.

"Good. Now I'm asking for the same chance you gave him five years ago. One night of intimacy."

She jumped up. "Kyle!"

"It's not as though we are strangers or looking for a one-night-stand. I want to marry you, Katie. And don't drag Aunt Bea and her God into this conversation. You are no more a God believer than I am."

He was probably right about the God thing, but for reasons she couldn't explain to herself or him, she couldn't go along with his request. Tears escaped as her eyes met his. "I can't, Kyle. I simply can't."

When he didn't respond, she moved out of his reach. "I'm tired. Will you lock up as you leave, please?" She hurried to her bedroom, locked the door and wept.

A soft tap interrupted. "That *no* includes Jeremy this time, doesn't it, Katie?"

"Yes."

"That's what I needed to know. Goodnight. Meet me at ten for breakfast." She heard the door close and lock.

After the reality check of last night, the atmosphere didn't seem half as intoxicating the next morning. "Sorry about last night, Katie. The fact that you are saying *no* to both of us gives me hope."

"Jeremy and I agreed to physical boundaries this time, Kyle." Her look was not accusing. Only informative.

He smirked. "Has he become one of those religious abstinence men?"

"He has been a believer since I've known him."

"Interesting." He stroked his chin. "Enough about him. This weekend is about us."

A competitive game of tennis and a visit to the spa melted any strain between them. After an informal lunch on the heated patio, Kyle escorted her to the suite his folks had reserved for a few more days. A knock brought Mr. Butler to the door.

"Come in, Son. Thank you for joining us this weekend, Katie." Though she knew the man was capable of strong emotions at times in the work place, he had never been anything but kind to her.

Mrs. Butler met them just inside the door. "We're honored to have you as our guest this weekend, Katie."

"Thank you for the invitation."

Mr. Butler indicated the young couple should sit opposite them. After general chitchat, Kyle approached the subject on Katie's mind. "Honey, I've explained to the folks that you have some concerns about becoming part of this family."

Katie took a deep breath and scooted to the edge of her seat. "Before we jump into those waters, I want to thank you for the most incredible weekend of my life. I will never forget it ... or you."

She reached for Kyle's hand. "Your son assures me that you know I am a single mom with a biracial son. I was eighteen and very much in love with his father at the time. I am not excusing or justifying JD's conception, but I am extremely proud of him and honored to be his mom." When she hesitated, Kyle squeezed her hand.

"If our marriage will cause problems or bring division to your family, I need to know now." She paused again ... knowing Kyle was unprepared for her next statement. "Although your son is willing to walk away for my sake, I won't allow him to do so. I have first-hand experience of ripped-apart families, and I won't be the cause of that happening to anyone I know and love."

Kyle jumped to his feet. "Wait a minute. That's news to me and I object."

"JD and I are a package deal. Either your family accepts both of us ... without reservations ... or our relationship ends here, Kyle. I chose him over my own parents' approval five years ago, and I'll chose him over yours today ... if necessary."

"Katie, I choose you and JD over them. Isn't that enough?" The look he sent to his folks spoke volumes, but she was not privy to its interpretation.

"Life is hard enough for JD, and I won't knowingly place him in a situation that will make it more so, Kyle."

Mr. Butler cleared his throat and reached for his wife's hand. "Our son's attraction to you has been no secret, Katie." He shifted to the edge of his seat. "We have no problems with your past indiscretion itself. The racial issue does present a snag, however."

The gentle giant rose as a roaring lion and confronted his father. "My chances with this woman have fallen dramatically since her trip to Asheville. If she walks away from me because of this conversation, I'll move to Denver and open up a business of my own."

Mrs. Butler burst into tears. "You can't mean that, Son."

He tempered his voice as he faced her. "I've never been more serious in my life, Mother."

The way Mr. Butler tented his hands reminded her of Kyle. "Son, Katie has asked for an honest answer, and I intend to honor her request to the best of my ability."

Between empathizing with Kyle and grappling with Mr. Butler's revelation, Katie was struggling to keep her own emotions intact. "Sit with me, Kyle."

He edged his large body close and placed a protective arm around her shoulders. "Tell her how narrowed-minded you and Mom really are, Dad."

A look passed between the elderly Butlers that spoke of unity. "Marge and I don't feel we are prejudice, Katie. We have some fine black friends and employees. However, it is our belief that the races shouldn't mix … romantically. It causes trouble in the families and makes life hard on the offspring … like JD."

Katie was surprised when anger didn't surface. She scooted out of Kyle's embrace and rose to her feet. "Thank you for being honest, Mr. Butler."

As she faced Kyle, tears comprised of more than one emotion began to trickle down her cheeks. "I'm begging you not to turn against your family because of this." She took his baseball-mitt-sized hands in hers. "You are a treasured friend, Kyle. I will always love you for that."

He jerked his hands away and stormed out of the suite without a word. Katie reached for a tissue before addressing his folks. "Be patient with him. Hopefully, one day he will understand the wisdom of my decision. Thank you again for an unforgettable weekend."

Before exiting, she addressed the Butlers one last time. "Jeremy says racism is a matter of the heart, not the skin. I agree, but I think the litmus test involves the mixing of the bloodlines. You use that as a reason to continue the division between the races. I see it as a bridge. What you perceive as a problem, I have experienced as an unexpected gift."

As Katie walked out of the suite and headed for her room, tears of release mingled with tears of regret. After packing, she called a cab and headed downstairs. As she neared the entrance, a valet drove Kyle's car under the canopy. A gentle hand touched hers. "Where are your other clothes?"

"I left them in the closet and the accessories are on the bed." She relinquished the case and followed him to the car. He handed her a small piece of luggage and a garment bag. "Get everything. My parting gift and I won't take no for an answer."

Sadness accompanied her. She was all too familiar with the fallout of rejection, and this time she was the cause. As she filled the bags, the tear flow increased … for him … for his parents … for JD. Fifteen minutes later, she rejoined him in the lobby. After the valet placed the items in the trunk, Kyle opened the passenger door. "I paid your cab. I'm taking you home."

Five minutes of silence spurred Katie to share the missing pieces of her story. "I know none of that makes it any easier, Kyle, but hopefully it will help you understand why I made the decision I did." Tears continued to drip.

Before turning onto Aunt Bea's street, he pulled into a cul-de-sac and parked. "Nothing is going to make this easier, Katie. My head hears your reasoning, but my heart knows that if you loved me as much as I love you, my folks wouldn't have the deciding vote. This is the moment I've feared since the day Jeremy Webster walked back into your life."

"Kyle, my love and concern for my son supersedes my love for you or Jeremy. As long as my personal decisions impact his life, his best interest will always determine the outcome."

The hurt in his eyes gave way to anger. "Bottom line? Jeremy wins. He not only regained your heart … he is the father of your son." He turned his face away from her. "At this moment, I hate him and it has nothing to do with his skin color."

Katie's snuffles caused him to shift and a softening came to his face. "You and JD are the only real people in my life, Katie. I needed the two of you to help me learn to be me."

She reached for the hand that was near her face. "Aunt Bea is real, Kyle."

"I'm looking for someone to share my life with, Katie. Not only is Aunt Bea too old, she is into God and I'm not."

"Why not?"

"God is a harmless placebo for poor, hurting folks who have nowhere else to turn. I'm hurting but I'm not poor."

He pulled back onto the street. When they turned into the driveway, JD ran to meet them. "Mama! Kyle! You're back. Are you going to be my daddy too?" he asked as he leaped into Kyle's arms.

"Afraid not, Buddy." Kyle let him slide to the ground. "Come on. Gentlemen always help ladies." He handed the smallest bag to his helper and manhandled the rest. Katie unlocked the door and stepped aside.

I'll mail the ring to you as soon as I get home."

After depositing her things in the bedroom, he walked to the door. "No. Sell the ring and put the money in JD's college account. It's just stuff and I have a surplus. It is people I'm short on."

A look of longing gave way to resignation. "I'm not accustomed to losing, Katie. I don't know where to go from here." His parting hug included JD.

When he drove away, Katie cried so hard JD ran next door to get Aunt Bea. By nightfall, she was calmer. "What about Kyle, Aunt Bea? He's hurt and angry … and I'm the reason."

"His heart will heal … if he learns to forgive."

By six o'clock the next morning, Katie was cleaning out the refrigerator. When JD woke at seven, she was ready to head south. They had said their teary goodbyes to Aunt Bea last night.

The five-hour trip, extended by an hour for pit stops and food, was a blur … except for the conversations she had with JD. He was asking questions she was not ready to answer. Katie had depleted her diversion ammunition by the time they turned into Wimberley Estates. Witnessing his delight with the residence she now planned to call home brought a sense of relief.

Before she could get the car emptied, Jeremy called. "You're home?"

"Yes, but you're not to …." She heard the dial tone.

Fifteen minutes later Katie watched his patrol car ease into the driveway. When she heard his key release the lock, she stepped out of sight. Footsteps indicated he made a beeline for JD.

"Daddy!" the boy shouted.

She heard their usual exchange and sounds of JD's sloppy kisses. "I missed you," Jeremy announced as he peppered JD with his noisy counter kisses to the stomach.

JD's giggles grew louder until he confessed. "Put me down, Daddy. I need to use the bathroom."

When she heard adult footsteps running her way, she jumped behind the shower curtain. "Did we make it in time?" Jeremy asked.

"Uh-huh. Now shut the door."

Jeremy closed the door. Katie didn't make a sound or move as her son emptied his bladder.

"Katie, are you hiding?" she heard Jeremy asked from a distant room.

After JD flushed and exited … without washing his hands … Katie sat quietly on the shower seat while the Webster men combed the place. "Daddy, where did she go? Do we need to call the police?"

"Son, I am the police. Do you think she sprouted wings?"

"Mamas can't fly, Daddy."

"Then we have to surrender." He picked up his son. "Okay, Katie, it hurts our male pride to admit it, but you've outsmarted us. One of us finds that rather embarrassing."

She quietly stepped out of the laundry room and snuck up behind them. "Well, someone needs a refresher course in sleuthing."

Jeremy casually turned around. "The lessons will have to come later. I can't stay long, but I need to tell you something." JD was clinging tightly.

"Last night Mama pulled out a yellowed piece of paper from her Bible and handed me Richard Bach's famous message about freeing those we love.

"I set you free last night, Katie. I love you, but if you've chosen Kyle, I'll survive ... not happily or without pain for a while, but I'll make it."

Before Katie could respond, JD interrupted. "Daddy, will you come back after work?"

His arms tightened around his boy while his eyes sought Katie. "If it's okay with your mama."

Those riveting green eyes held a sadness that was unraveling her resolve. "Why don't you come for supper around six?"

"See you after work, Son."

After JD slid out of his arms, Jeremy stuffed his hands in his jacket pockets and sauntered dejectedly out the door.

As soon as he drove off, Katie grabbed JD and headed for the closest fabric store. When they returned, she called Mrs. Carpenter. "If you're not busy, I could use your help."

"What do you have in mind, Dear?"

"Dozens of yellow ribbons around all the trees before Jeremy gets off work."

The woman's voice was energetic. "How exciting! My scissors and I are on the way."

What a fun time they had! Within two hours, the place had the feel of a celebration. Passing neighbors began to *honk* their approval.

Katie found her old record of the song that inspired the idea and played it for JD. "But Daddy hasn't been in prison, Mama."

"That's true, but he doesn't know we want him in our lives." Katie spent the rest of the afternoon unpacking and preparing Jeremy's favorite soup. Her emotions fluctuated between intense sadness for Kyle and a sense of anticipation for the three of them.

Now that her heart was free to love Jeremy ... she knew she did.

A look at the clock alerted her that the usually prompt man was late. "JD, let's get your bath finished before Daddy arrives?" After settling him in the tub with his toys, Katie went to the kitchen to check on the supper. She screamed as a hand grabbed her from behind.

"Katie, your front door was unlocked. Someone else could have walked in on you."

While she was taking deep breaths to get her heart back to a safe rhythm, Jeremy followed his nose into the kitchen. "Is that what I think it is?"

As the fear subsided, curiosity took over. The man could not have missed the yellow jungle. While she was considering the possibilities, their wet, naked son plowed between them. "Do you like the ribbons, Daddy? We did them all for you ... cause we want to be a family ... forever and ever."

Jeremy swept the little wet Webster off his feet. "The trees did have a yellowish glow. Who told you they were for me?"

"Mama."

A grin reminiscent of old times greeted Katie. "Is that true, Miss Williams?"

Her teapot stance was back. "Originally, but I think I've changed my mind."

He grabbed one of her hands and placed it on his chest. "I heard about the ribbons around three o'clock this afternoon, and my heart hasn't slowed down since."

"Who told you?"

"Detective Brownlow was visiting his aunt up the street and called me. I made up a dozen different scenarios ... all of which included Kyle ... to convince myself they couldn't be for me. That was when my co-workers locked me in a cell." Jeremy's eyes were searching hers. "Now my son indicates I was wrong."

"They should have kept you locked up." When she stomped to the kitchen to heat up the sour dough bread and add the clams to the soup, Jeremy whisked JD to his bedroom to get dressed. By the time the Webster men joined her, the table was set. Jeremy helped JD into his booster seat and then snuck up behind Katie. "What can I help you with, Miss Williams?" He lifted her long, thick braid and kissed her neck.

"Our boundaries are still in place. Keep your lips to yourself and get the bread out of oven."

Jeremy raised the lid and sniffed the soup. "Clam chowder? If I didn't know better I'd think you were trying to tell me something."

He jumped back just as she took a swing with the wooden spoon in her hand. Jeremy lost it when she began to mutter in Pig Latin. "Careful there, Sweetheart. Our son is listening."

Katie filled the bowls and set the breadbasket on the table. "I'm ignoring you, Sir."

"So, JD, tell me about your trip to Roanoke. Mama has developed a case of the cold shoulder."

JD was slurping his soup. "Mama cried. Aunt Bea talked. I played."

"Did you see Kyle?"

"Uh-huh. Him and Mama spent the night together, and Mama cried a long time when he brought her back home."

And that information was the source of Jeremy's uneasiness. Still she indicated the decorations were for him. After supper, he heaved JD to his shoulders. "Come on, Buddy. Let's go count the ribbons."

Katie had the kitchen cleaned and a warm fire going by the time they returned with cold cheeks and red hands. "Hot chocolate coming up."

JD succumbed to sleep around 8:00 p.m. As they walked out of his room, Jeremy pinned her against the hall wall. "Katie, if those ribbons are for me, then tell me what happened in Roanoke."

"Of course they are for you."

Before she could say anything else, he disregarded the boundary and kissed her soundly. "Now tell me about you and Kyle."

"I don't know where to start, Jeremy."

He led her to one of the sofas in front of the fireplace. "Start with the night you spent together."

Katie shared a brief synopsis of their time at the Hotel Roanoke. "He's angry and hurt and I feel responsible."

"Our wrong choices five years ago set us up for getting involved with him and Valerie. I hope one day they can forgive us."

"Me too," Katie said.

Jeremy pulled her to her feet and led her to the bay window overlooking the front lawn. "Yellow is now my favorite color."

She punched him. "It's about time you acknowledged that public display of affection." Katie watched as he exited the front door and wondered between the yellow-clad trees. He motioned for her to join him.

As she neared, he reached into his jacket pocket and pulled out a small box. Speechless was becoming a common reaction for Katie.

Kneeling, he reached for her left hand. "I'm five years late in asking. Will you marry me, Katie Williams?"

Tears pooled as she nodded.

"The ribbons shout of your forgiveness and love, Katie, but I need to hear it," Jeremy said as he slipped the ring on her finger.

The pools overflowed. "I never stopped loving you, Jeremy, but I couldn't see that until I was willing to forgive you."

"What are your thoughts about a wedding date?" Jeremy asked as he wiped her tears.

A blank expression shadowed her face. "Wedding? We haven't been engaged five minutes and you're asking about a wedding date?"

"Sure am. How about Saturday?"

She shoved him away. "Saturday? Have you lost your mind?"

"My partner says I have." He fastened his arms around her again and nibbled on an ear.

"Why so soon?" she asked as her heart and body warmed from his touch.

"I talked to my boss today and here are our options. The coming week, the week after Christmas or sometime next spring or summer … if we want a honeymoon. Otherwise, we can get married on one of my days off and forget a honeymoon."

Miss Teapot made her second appearance of the evening. "You know good and well I'm not honeymooning on the "V" woman's week."

"Yeah, the chief marked that one off the list."

"Saturday is too soon, Jeremy."

"Why?"

"I need time to adjust to the idea."

"I vote for Saturday, but I won't push you. Consider the options and let me know what you decide."

As they walked arm in arm back towards the house, Katie voiced a soft "Okay."

Jeremy stilled. "Okay *I'll decide* or okay *let's get married?*"

A sober, serious expression gave way to one of sheer delight. "The latter."

He grabbed her hand and began running between the ribbon-clad trees. He stopped and fingered one of the bows. "Let's save this one. I have an idea for the ribbon."

"I'll box up all of them. Who knows? We may need to use them again someday."

He held her loosely in his arms. "We'll apply for our marriage license tomorrow. Pastor Hudson will meet us at the chapel Saturday morning at ten o'clock. My folks and Mrs. C will serve as witnesses. The folks are excited about having JD for a week."

Katie quietened. "You made all those plans before talking to me?"

"Had no choice. Chief wouldn't let me out of the cell until I did."

She slipped out of his arms and untied the requested bow. "Let's take these down before the frost gets to them."

"Good idea. I'll get a container out of the garage."

As they were gathering bows, they began to discuss their future. "Where do you want to live, Katie? I've got a good nest egg set aside."

She turned towards her newly acquired home. "Would you be okay living here?"

"In spite of her actions, Martha must have cared for you, Katie. This place is ideal for a growing family." He glanced at her. "You do want more children, don't you?"

She nodded.

Jeremy closed the space between them. "Did you have a hard time birthing JD?"

"Labor lasted about eight hours but when they placed our son in my arms, the pain didn't matter. I had someone to love."

A sadness settled over his face. "I would have been there if I'd known."

"I know that now." Treasured and painful memories were bobbing around inside her head. "Aunt Bea called Mom and Dad to tell them about JD. Their message? *Give up the black baby and you can come home.* They would have accepted a white child, Jeremy."

A few tears found an outlet as Jeremy hugged her close. "Lord willing, I'll be there for the rest of our children's arrivals."

After collecting most of the ribbons, they settled in front of the warm fire and let the events of the evening soak in. Katie fell asleep. Unwilling to wake her, Jeremy leaned his head back and dozed. Several hours later, Katie stirred. "Oh, dear, what have we done?"

Jeremy kissed the side of her cheek. "Absolutely nothing except bask in our resurrected love."

Katie wiggled out of his embrace and off the sofa. "You need to leave now."

A crooked smile indicated he agreed. "Meet me at the county clerk's office at ten tomorrow morning."

"Still seems like everything is happening too fast, Jeremy."

"I'm ready Katie, but if you aren't, we can wait."

"I'm experiencing acute pain for Kyle."

"Is that why you hesitated?"

"Partly."

"I understand. Call me in the morning if you need more time."

Ten

Their visit to the county clerk's office triggered a variety of responses. None came as a surprise. The next four evenings were spent transferring Jeremy's possessions to Wimberley Lane. He spent the last hours tackling his first *honey-do* project ... repairing a dragging passage door from the kitchen to the garage and installing a more secure lock.

When he pulled in the driveway at nine o'clock Saturday morning, Katie reached for a ginger ale. She heard his key in the lock and then his excited voice. "Someone told me I had a wedding to attend this morning."

She walked into the foyer minus her jacket and shoes while slipping her earrings on. "Your best man needs your help."

Jeremy caught her arms as she turned to leave. "Katie, the girl I fell in love with was sweet and appealing, but the woman I'm marrying today takes my breath away."

She blushed. "I'm equally impressed with the man who will become my husband, Mr. Webster."

He kissed her quickly and hurried off to help JD. Soon the two of them were loading the luggage into Katie's inherited Honda rather than Jeremy's beefed-up truck.

"Daddy, I promise not to cry while you and Mama are gone, cause I want you to live with us forever."

Jeremy gave his smart son a big hug. "That's my boy."

Katie walked in on the tail end of that conversation. "What have you told this child?"

"Now don't get your tail feathers ruffled, Mama. We had ourselves a man-to-man talk. He understands how important it is to be a brave chap while we're gone."

Her left eyebrow arched. "Son, Daddy is going to live with us even if you do cry."

Jeremy breathed easier when the brow lowered.

"I do want you to be a big boy, but sometimes big boys cry. If you get lonesome for Mama and Daddy, you have Grammy call us. Okay?"

"I'm not going to cry, Mama. I promised Daddy." He clamped his arms around her neck and hugged her hard. "I've had you a long time. Daddy just wants a few days with you. I'm sharing."

He turned back to Jeremy. "We're buddies now, Mama."

A teasing, but equally challenging expression shaded her face. "Buddies, huh?"

"Lock up, Mama of my buddy. It's time for a wedding," Jeremy said with a wink.

It was a sweet ceremony. Pastor Hudson reminded them of the seriousness of the vows they were exchanging and spent a few minutes talking about the additional challenges of being a racially mixed couple. "God is looking for folks whose marriage is a reflection of His love. Yours will be watched by many."

When the ceremony was over, JD raised his hand. "What's my name now?"

A gentle laughter echoed among the adults. "You've always had your daddy's name," Katie answered. "Only my name changed this morning."

A huge smile emerged. "You mean we all match?"

Jeremy picked him up. "You betcha. We are now the Webster family." Folks offered congratulations and waved their goodbyes.

Jeremy had booked a cabin in a mountain resort outside Gatlinburg, Tennessee. The hour plus drive offered time for reflection. "Jeremy, tell me your version of the night we met."

"As I recall it was the annual rival game between Asheville and Erwin in the fall of 1988. I worked late that evening and by the time I arrived, the stands were packed. The only open space was beside a young, white girl with incredible blue eyes and beautiful, black, curly hair. While I was wondering what to do, our eyes connected and her magnetic smile pulled me in.

"By the time the game was over, I was wrestling with the biggest crush of my life. Not only was she white, she was only sixteen. The five-year gap in our ages was as bothersome as wondering what my folks and hers would say if I asked her for a date."

Katie's face mirrored delight and sadness. "I smiled at you because I recognized your face. Dad was a serious football fan and followed your career at Asheville High and the University of Tennessee. It wasn't unusual for him to read the newspaper articles … at the breakfast table.

"I thought he'd be thrilled that I had met you. He squashed that notion by letting me know in terms that I couldn't misunderstand that the fifty-percent black blood flowing through your veins made you off limits."

"Katie, until I met you, I never considered dating a white girl. By the end of the game, I was convinced you wouldn't be as beautiful any other color."

"I was in awe of the whole package named Jeremy Webster."

Jeremy cast an approving glance at his wife. "Loving you has convinced me God wants us to see the beauty in our differences, not pretend they don't exist."

She scooted closer. "Jeremy, Aunt Bea talked about having a relationship with God for five years. Kyle doesn't believe in Him and insisted I don't either. My folks took me to church but there was never talk of God in our home. I don't know Him like you and Aunt Bea do."

Surprise blanketed Jeremy's face. "I can't believe we haven't had this conversation before now. I assumed you were a believer, Katie."

"I believe there is a God, Jeremy; but I don't know Him. Are you upset with me?" An uneasy expression emerged.

He reached for her hand. "No, Sweetheart. I'm excited."

"Excited?"

"Yes, recognizing the need is the first step, Katie."

"What's comes next?"

"Getting honest with God."

"That sounds like Aunt Bea's religious jargon."

"Honey, just like you love and understand that boy of ours better than anyone else, God loves and understands you better than anyone … including me. Even if you struggle with the words, He sees your heart. Talk to Him like JD talks to you."

"Out loud?"

"If you don't mind."

Katie took a small, wobbly step of faith. "God … I think You must have saved that seat for Jeremy … because he is the best thing that's ever happened to me. I got real upset when he disappeared and my folks sent me away … but you already know all that.

"I find it easy to forgive JD when he messes up. I'm hoping you feel the same way about me. I regret Mama and Dad died with all the strain between us, but I'm glad Mama's death brought Jeremy and me back together. I'm working on forgiving them."

When she paused, Jeremy spoke up. "Katie, today we stood before our family and God, and with our mouths spoke of our love and commitment to each other. Marriage is another of God's earthly pictures of what a spiritual relationship with Him looks like. He's already spoken his vows of love to you by giving his Son to die for your sins. He is waiting for you to accept his gift and make your commitment."

Tears were now pooling in Katie's eyes. "How do I do that?"

"Tell Him."

"Lord, I do believe Jesus died for me and as much as I know

how … I commit my life to You." A few tears escaped. They continued the conversation the rest of the trip.

"Here we are," Jeremy said as they pulled into the Morning Mist Resort. After registering and procuring a map to their cabin, they approached a steep grade that caused mountain-born Katie to close her eyes. "I've been on some steep Asheville roads, but this feels more like a mountain goat trail. What if we meet someone?"

"Relax, Honey. It's a one way." He smiled as he downshifted again. "Where is your spirit of adventure?"

"I lost it when we drove by *the Eagle's Nest*."

When the car stopped, Katie opened her eyes. "What a place to spend my first week as one of God's new daughters!" Her gaze shifted to him. "And become your wife."

"Two new beginnings." He put his arm around her shoulder. "That makes this a very special place."

The cabin was surprisingly modern considering its location. Soon they were unloading luggage and food. By the time they finished, it was getting close to lunchtime. "You hungry, Babe?" Jeremy asked.

"As a matter of fact I am." She caught his eyes … and reached for his hands. "Why don't we eat later?"

"Later sounds wonderful." Jeremy swept Katie in his arms as they entered the marriage chamber prejudice and their own poor choices had denied them. And the two became one as God intended from the beginning.

Whether they were cuddling by the romantic fireplace, relaxing in the hot tub, grilling out on the deck, hiking on one of the trails with other couples or taking in a spectacular piece of creation, their Garden of Eden abounded with wonder and delight.

They were cuddling by the fire on the rainy afternoon of their last day when Katie posed a question. "Jeremy, Dad mentioned that you were biracial. Your parents are both dark. What's your story?" She felt him stiffen.

"Did he relay the rumors that surrounded my birth?"

"No." She moved to the floor in front of him.

Jeremy's eyes took on a faraway look as he stared into the fire.

"Twenty-nine years ago there was scattered racial unrest in our area. Some men began dressing up in tie-dyed sheets and terrorizing black couples in the rural areas. One night four armed men showed up at mom and dad's place.

"Two stayed outside. The other two forced their way into the house, tied up my dad and forced themselves on Mama. They threatened to come back and do worse things if the folks ever said a word to anyone.

"Nine months later, I was born. I have a white biological father somewhere in Buncombe County. Four white men know that. The rest of the world thinks my mom was unfaithful to my dad. I'm suspicious Mom has always known at least one of them … if not both."

Katie was crying. "Now I know why your folks discouraged you from marrying me."

He pulled her in his arms. "That's why I never considered dating a white girl until we met. I'm convinced God orchestrated our meeting and opened our eyes to see each other as He sees us rather than through the painful memories and prejudice of our parents."

Katie framed his handsome face in her hands and studied his captivating eyes. "Your mother is a fine looking woman, but I'm betting these green emeralds are clues to the identity of your dad. With DNA testing it's possible you could find out who raped your mom and fathered you."

He brushed her hair back. "That thought has crossed my mind more than once. I'd like to see the animals who raped Mom behind bars, but I've no desire to know the devil who fathered me. Sad fact is I can't know one without the other."

She snuggled. "Our children will have a father they can be proud of, Jeremy."

"Now if you don't mind, this is the last day of our honeymoon and I'd rather not spend any more of our time on such a distasteful subject."

She teased. "Your subject of choice is?"

"Love, Woman. Love."

Eleven

Katie knew it wasn't just the rain washing the forests and filling the mountain streams that occupied Jeremy's thoughts on their trek home. She waited quietly.

"Honey, when are you going to tell Kyle about us? I left Valerie a voicemail. I didn't want her to hear it through the grapevine. And when do we need to clean out your Roanoke apartment?"

"Kyle knew we'd marry." Katie traced the water trails on the side window as she gathered her thoughts. "Time is a strange phenomenon. The last month of my life makes Roanoke feel like a distant memory; yet closing that chapter is not going to be easy. JD and I will miss Aunt Bea and I'm sad to lose Kyle's friendship." Touching his arm, she added, "One trip in your truck before the end of November will take care of it."

"Maybe we can talk Aunt Bea into visiting sometime. Wouldn't JD enjoy that?" Jeremy asked as spray from a speeding car caused him to slow down until the rain and wipers could clear away the filmy residue. "By the way, when I called Dad to alert them we're on our way home, he said we need to pick up JD before we stop at our place."

Katie's eyes were following the rhythmic movement of the wipers. "Wonder what that's about?"

"No clue."

The sheets of rain pelting the earth when they pulled into his folks' driveway didn't deter Katie. Throwing a jacket over her head, she dashed to the porch. In seconds, JD plowed into her legs. "I didn't cry, Mama."

Ignoring her wet clothes, she smothered her sweet son with hugs and kisses. "I'm so proud of you." Looking into eyes so like his dad's, she asked, "Were you a good boy?"

"I was the *bestest* I could be."

Jeremy leaped onto the porch. "Got one of those hugs for me?"

JD jumped into outstretched arms. "Are you going to live with us forever now?"

"As long as the Lord gives me breath, JD." After a lengthy hug, Jeremy let the lad slide down his legs. "You've grown an inch. What has Grammy fed you?"

JD rubbed his tummy. "She is the *bestest* cook in the world."

Jeremy laughed and noticed his dad trying to get his attention. "JD, Daddy needs to talk to Papa. Why don't you and Mama gather your belongings?"

When his wife and son entered the house, Jeremy remained with Doc. "What's up?"

His dad's dark eyes stared at the porch floor where he scuffed his shoe back and forth. "Seems your marriage to Katie has stirred up some old hatred. They burned a cross in your lawn night before last. God bless Mrs. Carpenter. The officers said that woman was out in the middle of the night lecturing the hate mongers the entire time. It's a wonder they didn't hurt her.

"They've beefed up patrols in your neighborhood and things have been quiet since. Thought you ought to prepare Katie in case they show up again."

"They didn't wait long, did they? Any idea who did it?" Jeremy asked.

"None that anyone is talking about. Figure when you get back to work, you'll find out. You ever think about getting a good guard dog?"

"Thinking about it right now, Dad. I turned the other cheek when it was just me, but I'll fight for my family."

"I understand, but you be real careful that you don't do something foolish that will get you in big trouble." A strong, dark hand gripped his shoulder.

"I know … gentle as a dove but wise as a serpent." He stepped close and hugged the man who had loved him like a son. "You're the best, Dad."

Uncomfortable with the compliment, the older Webster lowered his head and stuffed his hands in his pockets. "We cleaned up as best we could, but Katie will know something has happened."

"She's tough, Dad. Life with JD has made her wiser than her years."

When they rejoined the others, Katie and JD had his belongings in tow. "We're ready to go home now, Daddy."

Jeremy swept the boy in his arms and reached for the offered umbrella. "Thanks for everything, folks." Katie followed with JD's travel bag.

Their son's constant conversation left no opportunity to inform Katie of the incident. As they turned into the driveway, the headlights revealed a large black spot on the front lawn. Katie's eyes questioned. Jeremy shook his head and pointed towards the boy.

As Jeremy prepared to open the garage door, he turned to Katie. "We need to install automatic openers."

After unloading and enjoying the supper Grammy had packed for them, they shared the evening with JD. "Will you be here when I wake up in the morning, Daddy?"

Jeremy pulled his son onto his lap. "I'll be here if you wake up in the middle of the night."

JD smiled. "I have a full-time mama and daddy now."

"Yes, you do," Jeremy said as he ruffled his hair.

Later that evening JD crawled over the side of the tub and reached for his favorite ship before plopping into the water. "Grammy showed me pictures of you when you were little, Dad. We look alike. Is that what makes you my real daddy?"

He looked at his miniature likeness. "Yes, God used mama and daddy's love to make you."

JD's eyes brightened. "How'd He do that?"

Katie walked in on that conversation and propped against the doorframe ... smiling.

"You know, Son, Daddy needs to get his uniform ready for tomorrow. Will it be okay if Mama helps you with your bath? I'll be in for story time." He rose from the side of the tub and exited with a sheepish grin.

"Be sure the chickens are locked up for the night, Dear," Katie said with a teasing smile.

After going through the nightly routine with JD, both parents quietly exited his room. When they reached the foyer, Katie turned to Jeremy. "What happened here while we were gone?"

As they walked to the great room, he relayed his dad's account of the event. "Seems Mrs. Carpenter gave them a hard time. That woman is something else."

"I guess our marriage upset the hatemongers," Katie said as she flopped on the sofa.

"That or they've figured out that a man of color is going to be living in a high-dollar neighborhood. How are you with dogs?" He lowered his body next to hers.

"JD has always wanted a dog, but our place was too small. I'd want him restricted to the great room, garage and enclosed area of the lawn. Is that okay?"

He nuzzled her neck. "Go to the pound tomorrow while I'm at work and see what they have." He got side tracked. "Have you noticed that JD has your nice ears and hairline?"

"So you are aware that he has a little of me mixed in with all those Webster features?"

"Does he ever talk about being different, Katie?"

"Only when a peer brings it to his attention. I hope he learns to appreciate the rich heritage both our races bring to him, Jeremy."

"Maybe he will become a bridge builder between the races, Katie."

She kissed his cheek. "I think that's what you are."

"Back to the dog. I'm interested in a good-sized dog known for its protective instincts. Sam is the caretaker at the shelter. Tell him to call me if he has any questions."

"Uh-huh, I will." Katie was messing with his hair. "JD has such beautiful curls. Yours are tighter, but I like them too."

"He got the best of both of us, Katie."

"Yeah, that's why everyone says he looks so much like *me*," she said jokingly as she kissed his nose.

"Anything in particular we need to get done before we call it a night?" Jeremy asked with a flicker of desire.

"As a matter of fact there is." Katie jumped up and ran to the master bedroom.

Jeremy grabbed his shoes and followed. "You in a hurry, Mrs. Webster?"

"Yeah, I need to make a pit stop." There was mischief in her voice.

Before he could walk away, he heard the shower water running and Katie singing. "Hey, that sounds like more than a pit stop … and wives aren't supposed to lock their husbands out of the bathroom," he shouted as he pounded on the door.

"Seems I have lots to learn about being a wife, Sergeant."

While she showered, Jeremy located his holster and pistol and placed them on his nightstand. He was looking for a spot to add a hook out of JD's reach, when he heard the latch click. His heart skipped more than one beat when his wife of one week walked out sporting a new negligee. "You make that kind of pit stop anytime you want, Honey."

With a shade of modesty evident, Katie glided into her husband's arms. "Didn't want our love life to lose its excitement just because we left *the Love Nest* … and added a son."

An endearing expression lit up his face. "That's not going to be a problem on my side, Katie."

The illuminated clock was flashing 1:46 when Jeremy woke out of a deep sleep. Reaching for the flashlight on his nightstand, he nudged Katie. "Honey, don't turn on a light. Dial 911 and report a disturbance. Ask them to keep the sirens off, but get here fast. Bring JD in here and stay put."

After slipping into his jeans, Jeremy grabbed his pistol and tiptoed towards the kitchen. As he neared the passage door to the garage, he heard voices. The intruders were drunk. He eased back to the bedroom. "Think you'd better alert Mrs. Carpenter to stay inside this time."

As he inched his body back into the kitchen area, he heard movement at the door and listened as someone tried to jimmy the deadbolt. Praying it would hold, he backed up and waited. Hearing them retreat, he slipped into the foyer and watched as three shadows crept by the bay window in the great room. Were they going for the double doors? Yep! Again, the locks and security rod held. They'd have to break glass to enter.

Spotlights began to crisscross the lawn, and three drunks headed for the woods at the rear of the property. Jeremy quickly turned on the back floodlights and exited in time to see Mike and Jeffery take one down. He stepped into the light and addressed the other two. "Stop right there, boys, and put your hands in the air. They kept running. When he fired a shot in the air, four hands flew up as two inebriated, white males turned to face Jeremy. "Hey, Jeffrey, I need two pairs of cuffs over here."

A wiry looking officer showed up, read them their rights and cuffed them. "Good work, Jeremy. Bet these are the cross burners." The arrested trespassers protested loudly as they were escorted to a squad car.

"I'll be back as soon as I let Katie know everything is okay." Jeremy hurried down the hall. "Open up, Honey." He smiled when he heard furniture being moved.

When the door opened, Katie lunged at him. "Are you okay?" Her hands were going up and down his arms, covering his chest and tracing his face.

"Sweetheart, I'm fine. We caught three burglars. There are two officers here. Keep JD with you and try to get some sleep. I'll be back when I can."

"It's happening fast, Jeremy." Her back stiffened. "I've got news for them. You and I are not going to run or hide."

"That's my girl." They shared a brief hug.

Twelve

Not only had the vandals keyed and spray-painted all three vehicles, they had covered the garage doors and interior walls with racial slurs. Two hate crime incidents in less than a week. Who were these people? A tag search of the impounded perpetrators' car gave one answer. Lucas Taylor.

"Did your paths ever cross?" Jeffrey asked.

"Afraid they have." Jeremy related general information. "Lucas was a couple of years behind me in school. Quite a track star and a smart kid with an attitude as I recall. My last encounter with him was Martha's funeral."

"Prejudice is ugly from every angle, Jeremy. Thanks to you, these three will face the consequences of theirs," Jeffrey added.

"Yeah, but what will it take to change their minds and hearts?" Jeremy wondered aloud.

"A miracle" was Jeffrey's response.

When the last detective left the scene, Jeremy slipped into JD's bed and caught a few winks in spite of all the traffic inside his head. Katie's soft whisper woke him. "Time to get ready for work, Honey." He moved aside as she placed their sleeping son in his own bed.

Katie listened to a recap of last night's events while Jeremy dressed. "All three are in jail for the time being. The car belonged to Lucas Taylor. They've probably identified the other two by now."

Katie grabbed the doorframe. "Lucas Taylor was here last night?" A visible uneasiness settled over her.

"Yeah. You know him?" Jeremy led her to the corner chair.

"I'm afraid I do." She began tracing the upholstery pattern on the arm of the chair. "Lucas and I dated, Jeremy."

Surprise reflected in his eyes as he tilted her chin his direction. "That's news to me."

"It was before you. We dated off and on my freshman and sophomore years of high school."

"You and Lucas? Talk to me."

"Underneath the veneer he wore to keep his dad off his back resided the potential for a great guy. Looking back, I realize I pitied him more than I liked him. We broke up the summer before I met you."

Jeremy was staring out the bedroom window. "Can't say I ever met the nice Lucas."

"His dad's prejudice rubbed off on him." Katie waited until Jeremy looked her way. "Are you aware the Taylors live in this subdivision? Even after we broke up, Lucas shadowed me. When he found out you and I were seeing each other, he was livid."

That news kindled fire in Jeremy's eyes. "Why am I just now hearing this?"

"I was afraid you'd confront him, and Dad would find out about us. I dated him several times while seeing you … trying to convince him that you and I were just friends."

"Were you ever afraid he would hurt you?"

"Me? No. You? I could never be sure."

He retrieved a uniform from the closet. "I want you to write down everything you remember about Lucas. Did Charlotte know about him?"

"Yes, I kept nothing from her except the night JD was conceived and my pregnancy."

Strong hands tugged her to her feet. "No more secrets, Katie."

She pushed back enough to get a clear view of his face. "Did you see Lucas and his folks at Mom's funeral?"

Jeremy inserted his pistol in the holster. "Yes, and now it makes sense. He warned me not to get any ideas about a certain white girl who was back in town." His mind was processing this newest information as he slipped on his watch and grabbed his billfold. "I'm going to ask Mom to hang around today if you don't mind."

"I'd enjoy her company," Katie said as she wrapped her arms around his waist. "Listening to the voices of prejudice robbed us of five years, Jeremy. I refuse to be swayed by their ignorance or hatred any longer. I'm not ashamed of us!"

He embraced his new wife with more emotion than he thought possible. "Marrying me has brought new troubles into your life, Sweetheart."

"I could say the same thing to you, but I'd rather face our troubles together than live without you."

He kissed her. "Me too, Mrs. Webster."

After Jeremy's partner picked him up that morning, Grammy Webster dropped in. A trip to the animal shelter introduced them to a six-month-old German shepherd. Katie notified Jeremy. Grammy stayed until JD went down for his afternoon nap. That gave Katie a chance to collect her memories of Lucas. Putting them on paper provided interesting insights into the man and their relationship. She had a rough draft done by the time JD roused.

Two hours later, the sound of a vehicle pulling into the garage grabbed her attention. A quick peek revealed Jeremy in a rental with a passenger. "Come greet our newest family member while I find a place for his food and bed."

Katie was accosted by the half-grown puppy the moment Jeremy opened the door. Abruptly his attention shifted from her to the passage door into the kitchen. Katie and Jeremy stopped and watched the magical connection between a boy and his dog.

"Let's take him to the great room, Son. Mom doesn't want him in the kitchen area," Jeremy instructed.

While the Webster men were getting acquainted with Ziggy ... so dubbed by JD ... Katie prepared the evening meal. She joined their laughter when Ziggy cleared the baby gates thirty seconds after they were installed. "Hmmm, looks like we have some training to do," Jeremy announced.

By the time Katie had supper on the table, the newest member had the other males charmed. JD barely ate. She gathered the suitable bones and scraps. "You and Daddy want to feed Ziggy?"

JD scampered off. When bath time was announced, he grabbed Ziggy's collar and proceeded to the bathroom. "I'll tell you what, Son. Every Saturday you can join Ziggy for his weekly shower. Okay?"

After unsuccessfully explaining why dogs don't need as many baths as little boys, Jeremy proceeded to bathe his son before tucking him in bed. "God, thank You that my daddy lives with us now. And thanks for Ziggy."

Jeremy added his silent amen and joined Katie in the hearth room where she was recopying her Lucas notes. He scanned the finished pages. "The officers working the case are looking forward to interviewing you."

"Do you ever wonder why some folks have so much hatred inside?" Katie asked as she finished the last page.

"Yeah, I do. My folks would remind us that Jesus prayed for his enemies even when they were killing him."

She softened. "You know I never once prayed for my folks. I was so angry and hurt that I wanted them to hurt."

"Let me show you something." He disappeared for a minute and returned with his Bible. "Listen to Jesus' words in Matthew 5:44. *I say, love your enemies! Pray for those who persecute you! In that way, you will be acting as true children of your Father in heaven.*"

Katie reached for the Bible and read the verse for herself. "That goes against our grain."

He tucked her hair behind her ears. "Yeah, it does. We want them to pay. And what is the result? More hatred and more violence. What if everyone ... I mean everyone ... got hold of this truth and learned to live it out? What would happen?"

Moisture collected in Katie's eyes. "Hatred and prejudice would cease."

"Don't get me wrong, Katie, I want Lucas and his friends to receive just punishment from the law, but more than that, I want their hearts to change so the cycle ends."

He reached for the newspaper on the end table. "Take a look at the front pages of the Asheville Citizen Times." A photo of the threats sprayed on the garage doors appeared under the headlines. *Local Officer Target of Vandalism*. The sub-title read … *Was This a Hate Crime?* The story was pretty close to the actual events and reported that Sergeant Webster had recently married Katie Williams." Separate photos left no doubt about the motive.

She shivered.

"You okay, Katie?"

"It's sobering to think about praying for Lucas and those two men."

They shared a hug. "I missed you today," Jeremy whispered.

Tipping her head to meet his gaze, she kissed him and wiggled out of his arms. "Take care of Ziggy and meet me in the hot tub."

Thirteen

Long before the alarm went off, Ziggy's deep barking woke the sleeping couple. Jeremy scampered out of bed to check out the problem. No intruders in sight. The newest family member wanted to play or needed relief. Jeremy let him loose in the fenced-in yard and crawled back in bed.

Katie stirred. "What was that about?"

"Not sure, but if this becomes a habit, we'll need to change his name to *Rooster*. Hopefully it's only an adjustment problem."

Both were quiet for a few minutes.

"Jeremy?"

"What, Babe?"

"I'm glad we didn't wait to get married."

When Jeremy's alarm went off an hour later, he groaned as he reached for the button. "I envy Adam. His life wasn't regulated by a clock."

"Do you think he left Eve alone all day?"

"Must have … otherwise she wouldn't have eaten from the wrong tree." He looked at her teasingly. "No fooling around with snakes. Okay?"

102 | JB PRICE

A huge smile emerged. "I'll leave those bad boys to Ziggy."

"Smart woman." After breakfast, he reminded her that his mom was going to drive her to Hertz rentals. "Things are moving along. I talked to Tommy at Farm Bureau regarding damages to the house and vehicles. They'll be cutting us a check for everything soon.

"After you pick up a vehicle, would you mind dropping your notes off at the precinct? Lincoln is eager to hear your Lucas story."

As was her habit, she was ready for the day by the time JD woke. Soon afterwards, Grammy was knocking at the front door.

"Come see our dog, Grammy," JD said as he led her to the patio.

While they entertained the dog ... or vice versa ... Katie cleaned the kitchen. "Those two are quite the pair," Jeannie commented as she came back in the house. "Do you leave him outside when you're away?"

"Yeah, he's happier outside than inside."

Little ears were listening. "Daddy says Ziggy can swim with me next summer. Isn't that cool?"

Later that morning, Katie drove out of the rental car lot in a minivan JD had selected and headed for the Asheville Police headquarters. As she and JD were approaching the entrance, Lucas and Herbert Taylor walked out the doors. Katie reached for JD. That was the moment Lucas recognized her. She considered turning around but quickly rejected that thought.

As she neared the entry, she realized she couldn't open the door without it colliding with Mr. Taylor's body. "Excuse me, Sir. I have business inside."

Lucas stepped closer as his eyes roamed over her body. "The years have been good to you, Katie. You should have married your rich, white, Roanoke boyfriend, instead of settling for a member of an inferior species. Your babies would have been thoroughbreds." Katie watched as his eyes shifted to JD. "Like father ... like son."

"Shut up, Boy." Mr. Taylor bellowed.

A boldness flooded Katie. "You folks still attend the Basilica of St. Lawrence?"

"Well, of course. Planning to join us?" Mr. Taylor asked sarcastically.

"Just wondered if the bishop has changed the message of God's love to one of bigotry and hate since I last attended?" The fire in her eyes went up several degrees.

About the time Lucas reached for her arm, the door collided with Mr. Taylor's backside. "Excuse me, Gentleman. I believe this lady is seeking entrance."

Looking the younger man in the eyes, the officer warned, "Lucas, your restraining order is in effect, and unless you want to return to jail, I suggest you move far away from Mrs. Webster and her child."

His nametag read *Ford*. "Thank you, Sir." Katie stepped inside the building and moved toward the closest chair. She held JD close trying to hide the moisture that betrayed her anxiety.

"Did those men scare you, Mama?" JD was wiping her tears.

Officer Ford joined them. "What did they say to you, Mrs. Webster?"

She repeated the conversation as best she could.

He motioned for another officer to join them. "Ma'am, would you mind if Officer Bennett takes care of your son?"

Katie was grateful for the help. "Maybe he'll show you daddy's workplace."

JD slipped off the chair and reached for the extended hand. "My daddy works here?"

"He sure does, Buddy." They disappeared down the hall.

She was trembling. "Thank you."

"Call me Walt. If you'll follow me, we'll get this done as quickly as possible." After she signed the statement regarding today's unexpected encounter with the Taylors, she handed him the envelope containing her notes.

"Katie, Jeremy is on his way and wants you to stay put."

She fiddled with her rings. "I don't think Lucas would hurt me." That was the moment she caught a glimpse of movement coming from the rear. Within seconds Jeremy had her in his protective embrace.

"I'm fine," Katie offered.

"Sure you are, Babe. Trembling and tears are part of your morning workout. I'm driving you home. Mark will pick me up in an hour. Where's JD?"

After she explained, he grasped her hand and headed towards the back of the building. Officer Bennett's hat wobbled on a pint-sized head as JD shared stories of Ziggy. When he spotted Jeremy, he interrupted his tale. "Daddy, two bad men scared Mama. Can you lock them up?"

Jeremy and Katie exchanged looks. "We'll talk about the men later. Right now, we need to get you and Mama home."

When they exited the building, JD pointed to their rental. "I picked the van."

"Thought you might. Let's try it out."

With the family safely back home, Jeremy and Katie sat on the porch while JD and Ziggy romped and wrestled within the security of the privacy fence. "Tell me about your day."

By the time she finished, Jeremy was pacing the porch. "Pray that he leaves us alone, Honey. The other officers are warning me to lay low and let them handle this. I'm trying. But if he harms either one of you, I'll have to take him down."

She grabbed his hands. "And what would JD and I do if you were in jail or dead?"

He pulled her close. "Keep reminding me of that." They heard Mark's patrol car pull in the driveway. "Will you stay home until I get off work?"

"Definitely."

"Lock the front and side doors. A couple of men will be here to install automatic door openers on both garage doors after lunch. I should be home before they finish." He kissed her quickly. "They're not going to win, Katie."

"I know."

Fourteen

Except for the crew installing the remote door openers, the afternoon was uneventful. JD took his nap and Katie tried to finish boxing and discarding the rest of her mom's belongings. She still found it hard to believe Martha left her everything. *Was this your way of apologizing, Mom?* Katie experienced a touch of compassion for the woman she had called *Mama.*

The men were finishing the doors when Jeremy drove in. JD was waiting for him at the door. "Mama wouldn't let me watch the men work, Daddy."

Jeremy picked up his son. "Smart mama. Want to see what they did?"

"Mama said we have magic doors now." His green eyes were dancing.

"Magic, huh?" As they stepped into the garage, Jeremy pushed a button on the nearly installed panel.

"Wow!" JD's face mirrored his delight as he watched one of the doors rise.

"Push the blue button," Jeremy said as he moved him within reach.

The door that had opened began to close. "They are magical."

Jeremy was grateful for the added security as well as the convenience.

As soon as JD was down for the night, Katie asked for an update. "Lucas has one or two drunk driving charges, but nothing serious. The other two have been in trouble since their teens. Both have spent time in prison. More than likely Lucas hired them.

"I called Mrs. Carpenter today. She gave us enough detailed information about the men who burned the cross that our people can now connect the two events. That woman's observation and memory processes are amazing. She described watches, shoes and even rings."

Katie reached for his hand as they moved toward the bedroom. "Are you concerned for our personal safety, Jeremy?"

"I don't trust my professional judgment where you and JD are concerned, so I have to take the advice of the folks working our case. They advised we stay alert."

As they readied for bed, Jeremy moved his pistol to the bedside table. "First of next week, we are installing a security system inside the house and possibly a few beams outside. My prayer is that we can put these people away before anyone is seriously injured."

Katie slipped into her nightshirt and turned down the covers. "In case you're wondering … I'd still say yes."

"Mark asked me that this morning, and I wanted to box his ears."

She rubbed her hand up and down his bare arm. "Love your brown skin, Mr. Webster."

"Mrs. Webster, I love all of you."

Mrs. Carpenter was feeding her cat when Jeremy took food to Ziggy the next morning. "Morning, Mrs. C. We had ourselves a quiet night, didn't we?"

A smug smile lifted half her wrinkles. "I moved into the bedroom on this end of the house yesterday. I'll have a better view of your place at night from here on out." A ringing phone interrupted the self-appointed neighborhood patrol. "Expecting an important call. Talk to you later."

Jeremy stared at the spot the spry senior had occupied. *Wonder if some angels have gray hair and wrinkles?*

When he shared the incident over breakfast, Katie chuckled. "Glad she's on our side."

JD and Katie stood in the passage door and watched the automatic door rise and close as Jeremy departed for work. "Come on, Buddy. Today we're going to transform your room into a boy's space." Besides changing out the curtains and bedspread, she had purchased a couple of shelving units for his toys and a table and two chairs for a reading and art center. By early afternoon, JD was perched in his new beanbag chair pretending to read a book. "I like it, Mama. Thank you."

When Jeannie dropped in unexpectedly, JD grabbed her hand before Katie could share more than a greeting. "Come see my new room, Grammy."

While those two were visiting, the door chimes rang again. Jeffrey and an older officer greeted Katie. Fear hit her with such force she grabbed the doorframe to keep from staggering. "What's going on?"

Jeffrey reached for her left arm as the captain moved to her right side. "May we come in?"

A dam broke loose. "Is he alive … or dead?"

The men guided her to the padded bench in the foyer and the older officer knelt in front of her. "Alive. He was transported to Mission Hospital. He and Mark were ambushed, Katie. Mark didn't make it."

Her relief that Jeremy was alive was diminished by the news that Mark's wife was hearing a different message at this moment. Sympathetic grief welled up inside. "God, help us all!" Cross burning and hate slogans were child's play compared to this. "I need to be with Jeremy."

"That's why we're here. Jeannie came to get JD. Grab what you need and we'll take you to him."

She stood but was so unsteady on her feet that Jeffrey called for Mrs. Webster. Together they helped Katie to the master suite. She grabbed Jeremy's pillow and sobbed. "Why, Jeannie? Why all the hate?"

Tears glistened as they trailed down Jeannie Webster's dark cheeks. She lifted her eyes and head to the One who knows and cares. "Father, out of the darkest night of my life, you formed a beautiful man child with the blood of two races flowing through his veins. Since the day he was born, Doc and I have prayed that in spite of the hatred and lust that conceived him, that he would become a bridge of reconciliation between the races. His love for Katie should not have surprised us.

"Now the same evil that conceived him seeks to kill him. We join Your Son's cry that still echoes in the heavens. *Father, forgive them, for they don't understand what they are doing.* I'm asking You to bring his assailants to justice, but more importantly ... bring them to their knees.

"Even now, bless the minds and hands of those attending Jeremy with wisdom and skill. Preserve his life and restore his health. Keep his heart and mind at peace. Give him a spirit of forgiveness.

"Help Mark's wife and boys get through this ordeal with their faith intact. According to Jesus, *There is no greater love than to lay down one's life for a friend.* Out of Mark's death, may a bountiful harvest of this *greater love* be reaped.

"Encourage Katie. Fill her with Your strength for the days and challenges ahead. Use what the enemy means for destruction as a platform for truth and love. Calm little JD's heart. Out of this tragedy, let Your glory shine. In Jesus name."

Katie had watched the woman pray. That was not religious jargon. Jeannie and God were acquainted. As iron sharpens iron, so faith encourages faith. After sharing a warm hug, Katie filled a small bag with a few essentials.

"The spare key is hanging inside the cabinet by the garage door, Jeannie. I'm going to go love on that man of ours while God and those doctors help him get strong again."

She walked into the great room where the officers were playing with JD. "I'm ready."

Jeremy's co-workers endeavored to address Katie's concerns on the trip to the hospital. Reporters and cameras were already gathering on the outskirts of the hospital. *Guard our hearts and tongues, Lord.*

Jeremy was in surgery when she arrived. After signing her name multiple times, they led Katie to a private waiting area. Trying to read magazines was futile, so she reached for the Gideon Bible on one of the tables.

Grateful it contained an index, she looked up the word *fear*. Isaiah 41:10 resonated in her spirit. *Don't be afraid, for I am with you. Don't be discouraged, for I am your God. I will strengthen you, and help you. I will hold you up with my victorious right hand.* The verses that followed talked about the demise of one's enemies.

A final check of the index led her to I John 4 where five words came alive. *Perfect love dispels all fear.* She read all the preceding verses again. Was it inferring that God's love has the power to boot fear out of our lives? She allowed the possibility of such a feat to roam through her fearful places.

After four hours of surgery, they transferred Jeremy to critical care and listed him in guarded condition. The surgeon's report was encouraging. Jeremy sustained a gunshot wound to the chest. The bullet missed his heart but hit his left lung. After repairing the damage, they put him on a ventilator to allow the lung to rest and heal for a few days. The good news? With his youth and health, they expected full recovery … in time.

Thank You, Father.

With Mark dead and Jeremy in ICU, their story hit the airwaves. *White Cop Dies Protecting His Black Partner.* Network crews were outside the hospital along with the local folks.

Katie called JD. "Daddy got hurt, Son. The doctors are taking good care of him, but Mama needs to stay here for a while." He promised to be brave for his daddy.

Two passages kept replaying in Katie's head. *Don't be afraid for I am with you and perfect love dispels all fear.* She wanted … no, she needed to experience that kind of love.

Jeffrey stopped by around 10:00 p. m. "You need to get some sleep, Officer."

"I'm on my way, Katie, but I wanted to fill you in on the latest and check on Jeremy first." After hearing the medical report, he shared the details now known about the shooting.

"Jeremy and Mark responded to a phony domestic violence report. It appears Jeremy took the first hit. Mark must have stepped forward to shield or help him. His body was covering Jeremy's. Neighbors reported the gunfire and backup arrived in less than five minutes. Our guess is the assailants thought both were dead.

"The house has been recently vacated. From all appearances, the perpetrators escaped on foot. Jeremy got off one shot and Mark unloaded two. At least one of them was injured. There are traces of blood in the grass across the street.

"Lucas and his friends are under twenty-four-seven observation. Chief called in federal investigators. Whoever they are, Katie, they will be caught. All officers on our force and in the county are taking this personally.

"Although the anger seems directed at Jeremy, an officer will escort you to and from the hospital. Chief said to encourage you to proceed with the installation of the security system."

In the midst of it all, Katie and Grammy Webster were dialoging about the level of hatred that could drive anyone to take the life of another human being. Grammy Webster encouraged her to ponder Ephesians 6:12. *For we are not fighting against flesh-and-blood enemies, but against evil rulers and authorities of the unseen world, against mighty powers in this dark world, and against evil spirits in heavenly places.*

"Does this mean there is a spiritual dimension to racism?" Katie asked.

"Yes, Child. When we seek to resolve such issues with human understanding and reasoning alone, we address only the outward manifestations of a much deeper problem. Behind every stronghold of evil is a spiritual root and until that root is exposed and removed, we won't find resolution."

Much of her time in the hospital was spent studying the passages

Grammy had shared that deal with God's solution to the ignorance and hatred that breed prejudice.

Except for Mark's funeral, Katie stayed at the hospital with Jeremy. On the fifth day, they began to back off his sedation medication and initiated a weaning trial. His response and numbers were good, so the weaning proceeded and by the end of day six, Jeremy was breathing on his own.

The first hours he clung to Katie's hand as though she were his life support system. Although her nearness calmed him, she knew he was troubled. His first effort to speak produced the three words she dreaded answering. "How … is … Mark?"

When she hesitated, Jeremy uttered. "He … didn't … make it … did he?"

Katie managed to wiggle onto his bed. Mindful of his injury, she wrapped her arms around her husband and together they grieved for his partner. When he quietened, she eased off his bed.

"You're making good progress, Honey. Tomorrow they are moving you to a step-down unit. Jeffrey and Mike are eager to take a statement … when you feel up to it."

"Sit." He patted the side of his bed. "How … are you … JD … my folks?"

A teasing grin surfaced. "Better shape than you are, Sergeant!" After medicating his cracked lips, Katie softly kissed him. "The new security system has been installed. No outside beams at this point."

Two days later, Jeremy was debriefed. Though his recall was clear and concise, he didn't provide any hard evidence about the assailants. That spurred his superiors to advise against returning to his house when dismissed from the hospital. Offering their in-law efficiency to a live-in, undercover cop pacified department qualms.

Crews had worked feverishly to remove all evidence of the vandalism while Jeremy was in the hospital. Katie sold her dad's Dodge truck, so Jeremy's newly painted Ford F150 would have a spot inside the garage.

Papa Webster helped Katie convert one of the four downstairs bedrooms with a private bath into a combination office and workout room. Beside the new desk was a large wicker basket filled with mail that had poured in since the story broke. She also added a pool table and dartboard to the hearth room. Her boys would enjoy those for years to come.

For security purposes, Jeffrey and Officer Bennett brought Jeremy home. She and JD were waiting eagerly. After hugging his legs, JD grabbed his hand. "We have a surprise for you, Daddy."

The officers said their goodbyes and helped the undercover cop get set-up in the efficiency. "Close your eyes, Daddy." Katie took Jeremy's other hand as JD led them to the newly transformed room. The wattage of Jeremy's smile was worth the effort.

"Marrying a woman with your talents has its benefits. I may not want to go back to work."

"Close your eyes again, Daddy."

Jeremy looked at Katie who again clasped his hand as they played follow-the-leader. "You can open them now, Daddy."

The look Jeremy sent Katie made her heart leap. When he reached for a cue stick, JD piped up.

"Look, Daddy. Mama bought me a stool and a shorter stick."

Jeremy moved to the sofa and patted both sides. "Come here, you two." An arm went around each as they snuggled close. "Having you in my life gave me extra incentive to get well." A group hug resulted.

The next day Jeremy asked Katie to add a small play area for JD in the man-space. "He's become my shadow, and I'm not complaining."

"He was brave those days he couldn't see you, but his little heart was fearful," Katie said.

She smiled as the list of officers checking on Jeremy grew as news of his workout room and new toys spread. Regardless of the reasons, their visits and mail call were therapeutic for Jeremy.

More folks were stepping forward to offer support to the racially mixed couple, including local ministers, priests and a rabbi. "Though the case is as cold as the weather, I see some good coming out of this," Jeremy offered three weeks later.

Katie was putting the final touches on supper. "I'm still shocked that Lucas is part of this."

"We have no hard proof of that, Katie. We know he took part in the cross burning and vandalism. We have not been able to connect any of them to the ambush yet. Right now Lucas is the model citizen, and his cronies have vanished."

Seven weeks passed and plans for Jeremy's brothers to visit over the Christmas holidays were on the calendar. "Keeping this rather large house clean is helping me stay in shape," Katie said as she patted his hand. "I'm excited about meeting your brothers."

"Don't get too enthused. Remember James wasn't pleased I married a white girl." He tugged at the two braids dangling down her back. "Have I mentioned lately that I like your shape?"

A playful smile emerged as she loosened the ties on her braids. "What would you think about a more rounded look?"

As she worked her hair loose, Jeremy studied her face and checked out her mid-section. "Are you pregnant?"

"*We* are pregnant, Jeremy."

Delight spread from his face like a strobe light on the dance floor. "Honeymoon?"

"Then or shortly afterwards. Haven't had a period since we married."

The sweetest laughter she had heard since before the shooting echoed through the house as they embraced.

"What's so funny, Daddy?" JD was tugging on Jeremy's shirt.

Releasing Katie, he pulled his son close. "Mama's pregnant, Son. You'll have a brother or sister in a few months."

A puzzled expression clouded the boy's face. "What does preg … what does that word mean?"

Jeremy took JD's hand and placed it on Katie's stomach. "There's a baby growing inside mama's tummy. As the baby grows, mama's belly will grow, and one day the baby will decide it's time to come out and live with us."

JD's questioning eyes looked at Katie's flat abdomen. "Did I grow inside you, Mama?"

She knelt as a tear or two made their way down her cheeks. "You sure did."

"How did I get in there?" He was looking between the two for an answer.

Jeremy drew him close. "Son, God put you there."

"Okay. I'm going to watch mama's belly grow."

As they snuggled that night, Jeremy rubbed her tummy. "Katie, this is your second pregnancy, but you need to remember it's my first."

"I know, but in some ways it's a first for me too. There's no fear or shame involved with this one."

Fifteen

Christmas holidays came. Raymond's family filled the upstairs rooms while James took the spare bedroom downstairs. Katie was amazed and delighted by the laughter and camaraderie that filled the house those three days. Jeannie and Doc did most of the cooking. She and Jeremy provided the sleeping and gathering place.

All visiting Websters left early Wednesday morning. Later that evening as they folded clothes, Jeremy expressed his appreciation.

"Best Christmas of my life, Jeremy. Did it dawn on you that I was the only pale face in the bunch?"

"Well, Paleface, you won James' heart … and that was a true Christmas miracle."

Between recovering from the ambush and the holidays, they had delayed the Roanoke trip. With Christmas over, they decided it was time. They left JD and Ziggy with the Websters and without notifying anyone except his boss and Mrs. Carpenter, they headed out. "Are you going to contact Kyle, Katie?" Jeremy was the passenger.

"I've not told you what turned the tide with him, have I?"

"Not specifically."

As accurately as possible, Katie related the conversation of that fateful afternoon. Jeremy pondered before responding. "You think he would have walked away from it all?"

"That's what he said." Memories crowded her mind. "I know now that Kyle's trust was in his family's wealth and power. He never saw a need for God."

When they pulled into the driveway, Katie dug out her old house key. Jeremy's face filled with remorse. "It's nice, Katie, but it's very small for a woman with a child."

"Yeah, this place was built with a single college student in mind. I was grateful to have it. Besides, we spent half our time in Aunt Bea's roomy place."

In the middle of packing and cleaning, they heard a car pull into the driveway. Katie hurried to meet the woman who had been a mother figure those five years. "Come on in, Aunt Bea. I want you to meet someone."

Jeremy was surprised to meet a very attractive, middle-aged woman. Somehow, he had an older, fluffier model in mind.

She extended a hand of greeting. "Oh, my. you're a grown-up version of JD."

He accepted her hand. "Thank you for looking after him and Katie those years."

Bertha smiled. "It blesses my heart to know God has put this family together."

Jeremy beamed. "We have a new one on the way. Due July 24."

"Making up for lost time, huh? Say, when you two finish here, come next door. We need to catch up."

After four hours of hard work, the threesome headed to Katie's favorite Chinese restaurant. Afterwards, they spent a couple more hours visiting. When the conversation died down, their hostess introduced a new topic. "Guess who's been showing up at my door since you left, Katie?"

"Not Kyle?"

"Yep! He's taken a leave of absence from the family business and has decided to move away. He and the family still talk, but he holds them responsible for losing you. I keep hinting that Jeremy had first dibs on your heart, but mostly I listen. He's a bitter man."

"Do you think I should call him?" Katie was clinging to Jeremy's hand.

"That's for you to decide."

Katie leaned forward. "Aunt Bea, how did I end up here … with you?"

Bertha fingered the cross pendant she always wore. "I met your folks years ago. They needed someone to talk to about your predicament. My efficiency had just opened up and the rest is history."

"Did you talk to them often those years I was here?"

"They called every month to be sure I got the check and to see how you were doing."

Tears filled Katie's eyes. "I've forgiven them, but it still hurts."

The chair stilled. "Child, there are lots of hurts in life, but God specializes in bringing blessings out of our messes."

Katie smiled. "You were one of my Roanoke blessings."

Warm hugs punctuated their goodbyes. As the Websters made their way out of town, Jeremy pulled into a rest area. "See if you have good reception on the cell phone."

"Three bars. What's up?"

"Katie, before you close this chapter, I think you owe Kyle an explanation."

She finger combed her hair and pulled it into a ponytail before letting it go. "What will I say?"

"Thank you." He stared into space. "He was also one of your Roanoke blessings. Do you want me to call him?"

"No, I will." Her hands were sweaty and unsteady as she dialed his office and asked for his extension. Mrs. Monroe's surprise was evident in her voice. "Just a minute."

Kyles' voice was guarded. "Katie?"

If the phone had a cord, it would be wrapped around her body. "Hi, Kyle."

Concern accompanied his question. "Are you okay?"

"I'm fine. Jeremy and I cleaned out my old apartment today. He suggested I thank you for being my friend."

"Thank me? That was the best year of my life, Katie." He paused. "I've been reading the newspapers. I could have spared you much of the turmoil you've experienced since marrying him. How's JD?"

"Doing great. He misses you."

Dead silence answered.

"Kyle, I never meant to hurt you."

"I've got a call on the other line." Katie heard the dial tone.

Tears rolled as Jeremy patted her arm. "Bitter?"

"Very."

Both were quiet for a long time.

Sixteen

W eeks passed without further incident. Jeremy returned to work, the live-in officer moved out and life for the Websters settled into a welcomed routine. As the winter months gave way to March and April, like the mountain laurels, rhododendrons, redbuds and dogwoods, Katie began to blossom.

"Cute little bulge you are acquiring, Honey," Jeremy offered as she put on her first maternity slacks and top. "You know I'm fascinated by the life growing inside you."

She kissed his cheek. "I've had to forgive myself more than once for not including you in my first pregnancy, Jeremy. I'm grateful we are sharing this one." They hugged as the blessings of today washed over the pain of yesterday.

That was the morning a local farmer called the Buncombe County Sheriff's department and reported finding the remains of a male body in a shallow grave on the edge of his property. Investigators and forensics spent the next two days exhuming the body and studying the surrounding area.

The local authorities were not willing to make a statement yet … except the man had suffered two gunshots wounds. One to the abdomen and one to the chest. Without public awareness, dental records of the men responsible for vandalizing the Webster house last fall were summoned.

Although Jeremy wasn't allowed to work the case, he was kept abreast of the findings. Two weeks later, they confirmed the bullet in the victim's abdomen came from Jeremy's weapon. The bullet to the chest matched the one that injured Jeremy and killed Mark. An all-out effort was made to find the weapon and identity of its owner. A possibility surfaced at a pawnshop in Weaverville. Harvey Perkins had purchased such a weapon a week before the ambush.

By week three, they confirmed the dead man was Clyde Murdock. The Asheville Police released an all-points bulletin for Harvey Perkins. When Lucas was called in, a high dollar attorney was present. The handsome playboy denied any involvement.

The month of June brought warmer weather and the opening of their swimming pool. As the heat of summer increased, Jeremy introduced JD to one of his and Katie's favorite summer places ... the Sliding Rock. Mountain water temperatures and an awesome natural rockslide offered the perfect combination for cooling down and hours of fun ... free. Sporting a life jacket, JD eagerly awaited their turn and climbed into his dad's lap repeatedly when it was time to careen into the seven feet deep pool at the bottom. Watching the videos Katie was taking doubled the pleasure of their first summer together.

Jeremy's addition to the video collection contained clips of Katie's growing tummy and the resulting challenges. "You do know there are fake baby bellies available for men to wear. Keep this up and I'll get you a nine-month model."

July arrived and Katie was determined to finish the nursery. A trip to Biltmore Square Mall netted her final purchases. As she neared her vehicle, she noticed an elderly man tinkering with his engine. His clothes were soaked with perspiration.

Feeling sorry for the old-timer, she unlocked her car, tossed her packages onto the seat and retrieved her cell phone. "Is there someone I could call to help you? This heat can't be good for you."

"Actually I think I've found the problem. Would you do an old man a favor and see if it'll start?"

"Oh, sure." She waddled to the driver's side and wedged her body between the wheel and seat.

"Okay, turn her on." It cranked, but did not kick in.

She could see him fiddling with wires. "Try it one more time," he suggested.

The sound of a smooth running engine brought a smile to Katie's face. That quickly disappeared when the man closed the hood. Brown hair peeking out the edges of the gray wig and a familiar face sent chills down her spine. The resemblance could not be coincidental. Harvey Perkins.

Don't panic. Think. "I'm glad your car is running, Sir," she said as she wiggled out of the seat and turned towards her car. "I'm late and my husband will wonder what's happened to me."

By the time she reached her door, he had blocked access and opened the passenger door to his vehicle. "You and I are going for a little ride, Mrs. Webster."

Remembering Jeremy's warning about getting in the car with a stranger, Katie struggled and yelled for help until he twisted her arm behind her. "Make another sound and I'll break it." He grabbed the phone out of her hand and tossed it.

Stall him. "Harvey, you're going to be in bigger trouble than you already are if you do something stupid."

While he was trying to figure a way to push her odd shaped body into the passenger seat, she succeeded in freeing her arm. *Draw attention.* She began waving and yelling like the clowns at a rodeo.

"Simmer down. Ain't nobody close enough to help you. He didn't tell me you were about ready to pop another black baby."

Katie stilled. "He who?"

"You can't guess?" He quit fighting with her and grabbed her door. "Look, Katie, I'm closing the door on the count of three, and if all your body parts ain't in, you and your baby are going to feel some pain."

At that moment, she saw a middle-aged woman exiting the

mall. Slowly she crawled into the car and rolled down the window as Harvey walked to the driver's side. When she stuck her head out the window and yelled for help, the woman started running in their direction. Katie opened her door. "He's kidnapping me. My name is Katie Webster."

Harvey walked back to the passenger side and pulled out a handgun. "Get in the car ... both of you ... and shut your mouths, or I'll bury you in a field ... after I air-condition your bodies."

Without another word, the stunned women obeyed. Katie moved slower than molasses in the dead of winter hoping for someone else to show up. Just as Harvey shut her door for the second time, a vehicle pulled into a close space. While Harvey was walking to the driver's side, Katie stuck her head out the window and yelled. "Help us, Sir. He is kidnapping us. My name is Katie..." That was when she felt the gun in her ribs.

"Another word and you and your spawn are dead."

The man was watching them closely. The back-seat woman rolled down her window and conveyed the same message. Katie made a decision. Dead was dead ... here or somewhere else. "I am Katie Webster and Harvey Perkins is kidnapping us." To her relief, he didn't pull the trigger. Instead, he gunned the engine and peeled out of the parking lot like he was doing a stunt for the *Dukes of Hazzard*.

"You ain't worth a dime dead, or you and your friend would be greeting St. Peter about now."

Though he drove like the lunatic she was convinced he was, that statement offered a fragment of hope. With any luck, the mall man was notifying 911.

Seventeen

Jeremy and his new partner had delivered a runaway to headquarters and were back patrolling streets when a kidnapping alert sounded. *Attention all units. We have a 207 in progress. An eyewitness reported a white male has kidnapped two white women from the Biltmore Square Mall parking lot. The suspect is believed to be armed. He is driving a black, four-door Chevy Impala. Last seen heading north. Pursue with caution. Units in pursuit identify yourselves. Unit 643 contact headquarters immediately.*

Jeremy and his partner were on Haywood Road. Everett responded. "Baker reporting. Within one mile of the scene. Advise."

Jeremy, Katie is one of the victims and she told the witness Harvey Perkins was her abductor. Back off and report to base.

Swallowing the fear that threatened to consume him, he took a deep breath. "Are any units closer?"

Three others are on their way.

"Are any closer?" Jeremy was straining for control.

No.

"That's my wife and baby. We are in pursuit." With police lights flashing and sirens blaring, Jeremy weaved through moderate traffic praying for a sighting. Never had he experienced fear of this magnitude.

Twenty minutes later. *All units. Kidnapper's car abandoned on Elk Mountain Road. Assume transferred into another vehicle. Closest units respond.*

Jeremy and Everett proceeded to the scene. "Any clues?"

"Yeah." An officer handed Jeremy the driver's license of Jayne Goforth.

"Everett, let's check out Katie's car at the mall."

Upon arrival, Jeremy noticed Katie's purse was in the driver's seat and two shopping bags in the other. He reached for the purchases … knowing what he would discover. Bedding for the new crib they had set up last night.

An officer showed him a plastic bag with a cell phone. "Does this look like Katie's?" Jeremy could only nod. *God, help her be smart until we find her.*

A call came from headquarters. *Jeremy, Chief wants you here. Information coming in.*

In the meanwhile, Katie had been trying to remember all the conversations she and Jeremy had about being a victim. When they switched cars, she crawled in the back seat with the other woman. Harvey didn't object.

The woman smiled. "My name is Jayne, and as crazy as it sounds I believe God wanted me in this car with you." She glanced at Katie's stomach. "When are you due?"

"July 24."

Harvey smirked. "You won't get to keep it. Lucas ain't puttin up with no black baby."

Katie placed both hands over her baby as anger surged through her body. "Lucas is responsible for this?"

"Who else would go to all this trouble to save you from the likes of Jeremy Webster?"

Boldness joined the anger. "Did he also hire you and Clyde to ambush Jeremy and Mark?"

"Nah, Lucas ain't got the stomach for killing. Somebody else financed that caper." He glanced at her in the rearview mirror. "I can't figure out if Pretty Boy hates Jeremy because he's black, or because you chose him or both. I ain't never seen him as mad as the day he found out you two married."

Good thing the back window was up. He rolled down his window and spit. Tobacco juice was giving her window the stained-glass look.

Jayne grabbed Katie's hand and began to pray … audibly. "Lord, Katie and I are in an awful jam. This man is listening to wicked voices and making some dumb choices for all the wrong reasons. It would help if You would disrupt his plans. And it probably needs to be now, rather than later."

Harvey added more detailing to the window art before speaking. "Look, Lady. You need to shut your trap and stop that religious junk right now. Reminds me of my mama. Always was quoting the Bible or praying some stupid prayer." He laughed. "Didn't do much good as you can see. Me and the old man didn't cotton to all that stuff."

That information lit a fire under her new friend. "Lord, I thank you for his praying mama. Sure would be a fine time to gather up all her prayers and tears and dump them in her son's lap."

He looked in the rear view mirror. "Am I going to have to tape your mouth shut?"

Jayne was on a roll. "Lord, rip the blinders off his eyes, unstop his ears and shine the light of your truth on all those lies that have his mind so screwed up. This man needs help more than we do."

Their abductor abruptly pulled the car to the shoulder and opened Jayne's door. "Get out."

She looked at Katie and then smiled at the man. "No, thank you. I'm going to stay with her."

He dragged her out, pushed her down the small embankment, and tore off down the road again. Katie prayed someone would rescue her unexpected companion.

"Got her shut up, didn't I? Lucas wouldn't be happy about her being with us anyway." He tore off down the road again while making regular changes to his tobacco artwork.

Katie wasn't talking to Harvey, but she was carrying on a lively conversation with the Lord when a call of nature beckoned. "I need to make a pit stop or things are going to get messy back here."

He looked at her in the rear view mirror. "Lady, can't you wait ten more minutes?"

"Nope. It's now or I'm not responsible for the outcome."

Her captor filled the air with evidence of his limited vocabulary before choosing words that communicated. "If Lucas wouldn't get so upset, I'd just let you mess all over yourself and this fancy rental."

He pulled over on the side of the road and opened her door. Katie stared at him. "You expect me to use the bathroom on the side of the road?"

"Look, Princess. It's here or in the car. Which is it?" When she refused the offered hand, he growled. "I ain't poison, you know."

"No, just a murderer and a kidnapper."

When she struggled to get out, he helped anyway. "Go over there in that tree line. I'll distract folks." While Katie waddled toward the trees, Harvey opened the hood and looked convincingly busy.

While attending to business she was trying to figure out a way of escape. While she lingered, an eighteen-wheeler pulled behind their car. Katie recognized the opportunity. *God, help me.*

The truck driver and her kidnapper were talking as she approached. When Harvey saw her, he slammed the hood, said something to the trucker and moved towards Katie. When the truck driver started walking away, she waved and yelled for him to stop. Her kidnapper warned the truck driver to mind his own business as he pulled her towards the open door.

"Get moving or you're dead regardless of what Lucas said. I ain't going to prison because of some dame." He pushed her so hard she flopped on the back seat. After another heated exchange with the trucker, he tore off down the highway.

Her efforts to straighten up sent a sharp pain into her lower back. *Not now, Lord. Please not now.* Thoughts of the baby's safety began controlling her behavior. She propped against the door and slowly pulled her legs onto the seat. Taking deep, calming breaths, she tried to relax. Thankfully, the pain began to subside. At some point, she nodded off.

The sudden stopping of the vehicle roused her. Unaware of how long she had dozed, she scanned her surroundings. They were inside a huge metal building with a fair size plane to her right. A male figure headed her way. *Lucas.* Anger and boldness unlike any she had ever experienced surged through her body.

When the creep opened her door and offered his hand, she slapped it away. "Come on, Honey. I know you're upset with me right now, but when you learn the truth about your Jeremy, you'll thank me."

"Don't you *Honey* me, Lucas Taylor."

When she crossed her arms and refused to move, he tried to lift her out. "I need you to cooperate, Sweetheart. Information has come to light that will change our future forever."

Dagger eyes pierced him. "You've done some stupid things, Lucas, and your dad has bailed you out of them all. Even he won't be able to save you from this level of stupidity. Have you lost your mind?"

"Now Katie, I've put a lot of thought into this rescue plan." He scratched his head. "Can't understand how folks figured out I was the mastermind though."

"Rescue? There goes *stupid* again, Lucas. Taking someone against their will is called kidnapping." She waited until she had his full attention. "I'll tell you how folks found out. Jayne."

"Who the blazes is Jayne?" He asked while making another effort to remove her from the vehicle.

Crossed arms and stiff legs with a rounded center frustrated another attempt. "Oh, she would be the other kidnapped lady who heard Harvey's confession about ambushing Mark and Jeremy and your plans for kidnapping me … before he booted her out of the car."

The man's face turned crimson and the veins in his neck resembled ropes. He abruptly turned and disappeared. If she didn't have to use the bathroom again, she would have stayed put. Seemed like a good spot to negotiate and buy time. However, her bladder beckoned.

She scooted out of the car and began to shuffle around the building looking for a restroom sign. Seeing nothing, she headed for a section that had the appearance of an office. A young woman who reminded her of Daisy Duke was sitting at the desk.

"What can I do for you, Honey?" Even sounded like Daisy.

"I need to use the restroom, but more importantly, my name is Katie Webster and Lucas Taylor is trying to kidnap me. Please call the police and tell them where I am."

When Daisy pointed, Katie waddled through the door that promised relief. After accomplishing her business, she lowered the lid and sat down to think. The room had no windows, so she couldn't escape or yell for help. She didn't have anything to write with which ruled out leaving a message. She could only pray that Daisy had believed her story and was phoning the authorities.

She remembered Jeremy talking about creating a disturbance or doing something to draw attention. Difficult to do in a room barely big enough to serve its purpose. The only thing possible was to stop up the sink and turn on the water ... full force. She had no idea how it could help, but it made her feel like she was doing something.

As the sink began to run over, Lucas knocked on the door. "Honey, are you okay? We need to be leaving soon."

She didn't answer or move. Where was Daisy? Were the police on their way?

He knocked again ... louder this time. "Katie, you need to come out. We have connections to make."

She heard him talking to Daisy but couldn't distinguish the words due to the rush of water cascading from the sink and pooling on the floor. Maybe she should turn off the faucet. Nah.

A knock that hinted of anger drew her attention. "No more games, Katie. Either you open up or I'm going to break this door down. And you'd better be out of the way when I do."

As he started his countdown, she backed into the corner and reached for the doorknob. "One ... two." The second before he said *three,* she turned the knob and jumped back. The force of his thrust combined with the wet floor sent him head first into the mirror. The next instant his feet slid out from under him as his arms tried to catch air. That's when the back of his head collided with unyielding concrete.

She stared for a few seconds before stepping over his prone, still body and headed for the exit door. A brief glance at Daisy gave her hope. *I called,* she mouthed. A young mechanic with his cap on backwards had joined the gathering.

When Katie reached for the doorknob, an angry, wet Lucas with a doozy of a goose egg forming on his head grabbed her arm. If this wasn't a serious situation, she would have laughed.

"Now, I know you're afraid of flying, Honey, but your folks want to see you before the baby comes." He glanced at the two strangers who were taking in every movement and word.

Katie tried to pull away. "I am not your wife or your honey. My parents are both dead and you are trying to kidnap me. Now these two know the truth. What are you going to do? Kidnap all of us?"

Smiling and talking while gritting one's teeth is difficult, but Lucas proved it's doable. "Now Sweetheart, we don't need to get these two young folks involved in our family disagreements."

She shoved him so hard he tripped over Cooter's toolbox. "Disagreements! Lucas Taylor, that's the story of our relationship. Now you get out of this office and leave me alone, or I'm going to call the police."

He scrambled to his feet and swept her off hers. Looking rather helpless, he nodded to the young man. "Would you mind opening the door for us?"

Shoving his cap to the back of his head, Cooter spit out the side of his mouth. "Nah. I'm rather enjoying this little show."

Katie shot a look at the local mechanic that would have alerted a more discerning person. "Hey, this man is trying to kidnap me. Bet his face is all over the news by now. Might even be a reward in it for you. Don't open the door. Tackle him!" And she started squirming and making it difficult for Lucas to hold on to her odd shaped body.

He and she froze as the sound of sirens surrounded the building. Lucas put her down and pointed the hard object she had felt pushing in her side at the two innocents caught in the fracas. "You two get in the bathroom and don't move or speak."

Cooter looked at Daisy Mae. "Well, I'll be. She was telling the truth." Daisy grabbed him by the shirtfront and pushed him into the bathroom. The door wouldn't shut, so they just stood there ... staring wide-eyed at Lucas and Katie.

With the gun in Katie's ribs, Lucas pushed her out the door. "Now, Princess, walk toward the plane and climb those steps. I'm willing to bet they'll let us fly out of this place."

Patrol cars and men with guns were everywhere. The severity of his crime and her situation finally registered.

The plane was plush. He led her to a seat and ordered the pilot to start the engines and move to the runway.

"Sir, I'll try." The engines revved as the pilot went through his checklist. When the plane stopped about half way out of the hanger, Lucas questioned the delay. "Mr. Taylor, there are three patrol cars in my path and about a dozen guns aimed at my head."

"Get me in touch with the control tower," Lucas demanded. The pilot talked to a couple of folks and then handed the head set to Lucas.

"Patch me through to Jeremy Webster. This is Lucas Taylor and I have Katie."

The chief of police and Jeremy had boarded a helicopter in Asheville and were following the trail as tips came in. The truck driver had not only called in the mishap, but also followed the car to the Tri-Cities Regional Airport. The tip from Daisy Mae had pinpointed their location and given them time to place their own pilot in Lucas' plane. The last report indicated Katie was in the hangar with Lucas.

Lucas' demand was conveyed to the Chief. "Put him through." Randolph nodded to Jeremy.

"Webster here."

After calling Jeremy a few choice words reserved for those of mixed races, Lucas continued. *Katie is with me and that's where she is going to stay. If you don't get these cars out of my path and those guns pointing somewhere else, there will be three dead people on this plane. I'm not going to prison, and I refuse to allow her to come back to you. Your choice, Black Boy.*

Jeremy looked at the chief. "Stall him."

"Hey, I'm a peon. I can't call this off." He was struggling to keep his voice steady.

Lucas laughed. *Wrong answer, Poster Boy. You've become a national celebrity. Now get them out of my way or else.*

"Lucas, you hurt Katie or my baby and I'll hunt you down."

I have no intention of hurting Katie. I'm rescuing her from you, and in a couple of weeks she'll let the world know I'm telling the truth. So what is it? I'll give you fifteen minutes to convince these uniforms to clear a path for us.

"I'll do what I can, Lucas."

The chief was checking with the airport. "Can you communicate with the pilot without Lucas hearing you?"

Affirmative. Pilot now wearing the headset.

"Patch me through."

Captain Nelson.

"Captain, this is Chief Randolph of the Asheville Police Department. Jeremy Webster and I are en route to the airport. Stall as long as you can."

Ten four.

"Are you carrying the sedation powder for neutralizing a combative passenger?"

Affirmative.

"If you can't stall, head to the Asheville Airport. They are aware of your situation. If between take off and there, you're able to disable the subject, notify us immediately. We're going to trail you. How is Katie?"

Captain Nelson chuckled. *Feisty. Lucas is currently in the restroom changing out of his very wet clothes. He has matching pump knots on the front and back of his head plus a bum knee. Makes me wonder how much damage she could inflict if she wasn't pregnant.*

Jeremy managed a weak smile. "That's my girl!"

Lucas returned. "So what is it? Are they going to let us fly out of here?"

"They're working it out. Mr. Taylor," the pilot offered as he checked his instruments again. "Captain Nelson requesting clearance for takeoff."

Permission granted. Proceed to the runway.

As they prepared for takeoff, Lucas took the seat opposite Katie. "Looks like Jeremy has more clout than he realized."

"Lucas, why are you doing this?"

"Why? Besides Jeremy stealing my girl, I've heard some news that is going to change our lives." He leaned back and reached for a thermos. "Want a drink?"

Unsure what he was offering, she made a different request. "Do you have milk or water?"

He fetched her a cold carton of milk and a bottle of cold water. "Are you hungry?"

She nodded as she downed half a bottle of water before placing it in the holder on the side of her seat. He left again and returned with a wrapped sandwich and an apple for both of them. As she ate, she studied the enigma called Lucas. "We broke up before I met Jeremy. Why can't you let it go?"

He took a couple of bites of his sandwich before answering. "Did you know our dads were best friends?"

"Herbert Taylor and my dad? No way."

"Your dad came to our place all the time. Said your mom didn't approve, but she knew to keep her mouth shut. For some reason he didn't want you to know."

Katie chewed the bite in her mouth while ruminating on the new information.

Lucas rubbed the back of his head again. "Holy moly, are you in for a surprise! My old man told me a family secret a couple of months ago that involves your dad." He scooted closer. "Your dad knew Jeremy was the father of your baby. That's why he shipped you off. Tore him up because you chose a black baby over him. Said he never wanted to see you again."

Tears filled her eyes. "He didn't."

Lucas leaned forward. "You ever wonder why Jeremy's folks are so dark and he's a light black?"

Katie made every effort to remain calm outwardly although her internal systems went on full alert. "Why don't you tell me, Lucas?" As the plane lifted, her baby grew more restless. Her hands instinctively moved to calm the little one and hopefully herself.

"Seems Jeremy's mama liked white men when she was young, especially your daddy. My dad said except for her skin color, Jeannie Webster was one of the finest looking women in the county in those days. No one knows exactly how it happened, but she seduced your dad and nine months later, Jeremy was born. He is your half-brother, Katie."

Katie looked away to keep Lucas from seeing the impact his story was having. Was her dad one of the men who raped Jeannie? Was her husband also her half-brother? How did Herbert Taylor know that information?

Considering those possibilities turned her stomach into a churning machine. She started scooting to the front of her seat and pushed herself awkwardly into a standing position. "Excuse me, Lucas. I'm going to be sick."

Holding to the seats as she moved to the restroom, she made it inside before losing what little food she had eaten today. *My father raped Jeannie? Jeremy is my brother?*

A soft knocking came to the door. "Are you okay, Katie?"

"No, Lucas, I'm not." She used the facilities and washed her face as well as her hands before opening the door. He was standing close by.

"Now you understand that I'm rescuing rather than kidnapping you." The man was serious. She pushed past him and took her seat again.

"Do you want to hear the rest of the story?"

"I can't take any more news today, Lucas. I'd like to brush my teeth and take a nap."

Lucas disappeared for a few minutes and returned with a toothbrush and toothpaste. "A thank you would be nice." His eyes caught her attention. Had they always been that green? Green! *Sweet angels in heaven*, she uttered under her breath as she fanned her hot face with her hands.

Her dad's eyes were sky blue like hers, not emerald green. Her heart was racing while her mind was processing information faster than the New York Stock Exchange. She was taking mental notes of every facial feature and the body shape of this man who had been a thorn in her flesh for years.

"Why are you staring at me like that? Is the knot on my head getting worse?" He lightly fingered the swelling.

Was this Jeremy's half-brother instead of hers? Was Herbert Taylor the other man who raped Grammy? Lucas' eyes were mirrors of Jeremy's. The longer she looked at him the more physical likeness she saw. Another wave of nausea hit and she started maneuvering to the edge of her seat. "Excuse me, Lucas. I feel sick again."

This time she accepted his help. Once inside she heaved until she was weak. She tried to shut down the implications of what he had said, but couldn't. A deep breathing exercise helped but only momentarily. She leaned against the door … praying for a sense of calmness.

A soft tap startled her. "Katie, I'm worried about you."

She opened the door. "You wouldn't have any ginger ale, would you?"

"No, but I'll be sure we pick up some at our first stop." He put his arm around her waist and helped her back to her seat. "You're trembling. I'm sorry you had to hear the news from me, but you needed to know the truth."

"Lucas, would you mind if I turn off my light and recline my chair? I'm not feeling well." She was trying to get comfortable when he brought her a small pillow and soft coverlet. She closed her eyes hoping her mind would settle down, so her body and the baby could rest.

"Thank you."

When he kissed her cheek, her eyes popped open, and she instinctively slapped his face so hard her fingerprints lingered. "I am a married woman and I'll thank you to keep your hands and lips off me. Leave me alone, Lucas. Leave … me … alone."

The muscles in his face tightened. "Have you not heard a thing I've said? Jeremy is your half-brother … which means your marriage is illegal … and your poor children will be half-wits."

"Get out of my sight, Lucas. Understand. Go … away." She pulled the cover over her face.

The baffled man moved to the front of the plane.

"The lady sounds a little miffed," the pilot said.

Lucas rubbed his cheek and rolled his head from side to side before responding. "She's always been spirited. Think that's one of the reasons I've liked her so much."

His hands were assessing the size of the knots on his head. "You wouldn't have anything for a headache, would you?"

The pilot reached inside his jacket and pulled out a package that resembled a *BC Headache Powder.* "Guaranteed to cure what ails you."

Lucas reached for the packet, mixed it in a bottle of water and gulped it down. "How long does it take before this stuff works?"

"About ten or fifteen minutes and you won't feel a thing."

"Thanks. I'll keep some around from here on out. That woman can be a headache at times." He half laughed.

In fifteen minutes, Lucas was out cold. The pilot called the Asheville Airport to alert the authorities that the subject was subdued, and he would be arriving in five minutes.

That information was patched through to the chief. The tears Jeremy had stuffed down all day broke through. "She's safe. Thank God! How far to the airport?"

"We're about five minutes behind them." The chief contacted his department who had officers on standby at the airport.

"Will the drug keep him down that long?" Concern edged Jeremy's question.

The chief laughed. "We'll have him safely tucked away in jail before he wakes up. Don't worry. It's over."

The pilot called Katie over the speaker system. "Mrs. Webster, this is the captain. Can you come to the front, please?"

Katie stirred. When he called her name the second time, she edged out of her seat and slowly made her way to the front. "What happened to him?" she asked as she peered at Lucas' limp body.

"He's been drugged and will be out for several hours. We're waiting to land. I just received word that your husband will be meeting you. The ordeal is over, Ma'am."

Katie slumped into the seat next to Lucas. The relief that flooded her body left her as limp as he looked. She studied him again. Could *he* be Jeremy's half-brother? DNA was the answer. She had to talk with Grammy Webster first.

"Buckle up, Mrs. Webster. We've been approved for landing." As soon as he taxied to a stop and turned off the engines, Captain Nelson opened the door. A swarm of officers rushed onto the plane. One assisted her. The others frisked the sedated kidnapper.

"Hey, look at this. His pistol is empty. No bullets on his person either but take a look at those goose eggs."

An officer escorted Katie to a waiting vehicle where Captain Jones, head of airport security waited. "I've been told to hold you here until your husband arrives. I believe that's their helicopter approaching now."

Katie was taking deep breaths ... trying to stay calm as she watched Jeremy's helicopter land next to the plane she had exited.

When she saw him duck under the blades, tears and laughter mingled. When Captain Jones helped Katie out of the vehicle, Jeremy broke into a sprint. In seconds, he had her in his arms. "You okay, Katie?"

"I am now." There were more tears than words.

The captain drove the car beside them. "Can I get you two anything before they take you home?"

Jeremy offered his hand to the captain. "I think we'll rest in your car if you don't mind, Sir." After tucking Katie in, Jeremy opened the door on the other side and slid close. The captain excused himself.

"Come here, Woman." He pulled her into his arms and gently reached one hand down and caressed their baby. "I've never been as scared in my life."

"I was petrified until Harvey spilled the beans about Lucas not wanting me harmed. That gave me the courage to resist. I kept going over all those talks we've had."

He laughed and hugged her again. "I heard you were a rather feisty captive."

"Thankfully, crime is not Lucas' field of expertise. I did learn that he had nothing to do with the ambush. Someone else hired Harvey and Clyde."

Jeremy catalogued that bit of information and brushed her hair away from her face. "Would you still marry me, Katie?"

"Yes."

Someone was tapping on the window. "Ready to head home? Don't know about you, Katie, but your other half hasn't eaten all day," the captain offered.

"Something disrupt your day, Sergeant?" Katie teased.

Jeremy grinned as he helped her out of the car. "Yeah, my wife was flitting around the country with another man."

She leaned into his embrace as they walked to the patrol car. "Lesson learned, Sir."

The ordeal itself was over, but Katie's hunches were gathering steam.

Eighteen

Katie fell asleep on the sofa while Jeremy was tucking JD in for the night. As he carried her to their bed, he recalled the last few hours. They had much to talk about, but it would have to wait.

Although Katie was up during the night, she slept late the next morning. In fact, they all did. A little after 8:00 a.m. JD stumbled into their bedroom and snuggled close to his mom. "Little Brother, can you hear me? I'm glad you and Mom are back. Isn't it about time for you to come out?"

"It won't be long," Katie assured him.

JD looked at her face and then the rounded mound. "Mom, you're not going to pop open, are you?"

She laughed. "Sometimes, it feels like it, but no, I promise I won't pop."

JD crawled onto Jeremy's back as he rose from the bed.

"I'll get this curious child some breakfast while you get dressed. Chief is eager to talk to you about your ordeal."

"I'd like for you to be there if possible. Think your folks can take care of JD or do I need to call Charlotte?" Her exit from the bed was less than graceful.

"Mama, did I make you fat?"

She looked at Jeremy and then her son. "Yes, JD. I was bigger with you than this baby."

His eyes enlarged and his mouth dropped open. "Do you remember that, Dad?"

Katie diverted his attention. "Come quickly, you two. Put your hands here."

JD's hand gently touched her tummy. "He's kicking again, Mama."

Placing her hand over her son's she added, "You know, JD, this may be a little girl."

With an endearing look of maturity, he answered. "Yeah, Daddy and I talked about that. We won't send her back."

A quiet laugh escaped. "Well, I'm glad to hear that. You two go eat some breakfast. I'll be in soon."

After breakfast, they dropped JD off at the Websters and headed to the police department. After several episodes of hesitation during the debriefing, the chief turned off the recorder. "Katie, is there something you want to say off the record?"

"I'd like to talk to Jeremy privately for a few minutes."

Chief Randolph rose and nodded to the detectives working the case. When the door closed, Jeremy scooted his chair close. "Did Lucas or Harvey do anything to you, Katie?"

"It's not what they did, but what Lucas said. I wanted to talk to your mom privately before talking to you or the police, but maybe I need to tell you first."

She rose from her chair and wondered around the room. "Jeremy, I think I know the men who raped your mom, and that means one of them is your biological father."

Jeremy jumped out of his chair and confronted her. "What did he say?"

She repeated Lucas' story, then she put her hands on his arms. "Pretend that I've never seen Lucas Taylor and give me a good police description of him."

Jeremy backed away and gave her a puzzled look. "Well, he's

about six feet, two or three inches tall. I'd say he weighs around two hundred and twenty … give or take a few pounds. Has dark, curly hair, a strong jaw-line with a deep cleft in his chin, straight nose, full lips, dark, arched, bushy eyebrows, and nice white teeth."

He was thinking. "His ears are tucked close to his head, but for the life of me I can't remember the color of his eyes."

Katie stepped in front of him. "They are replicas of yours. Except for the color of your skin and your nose, you've pretty much described yourself. Add that to what he was saying about the secret Herbert told him and I'm convinced that he was one of the men who could be your father. Can the department legally run a DNA test on Lucas while he is incarcerated? If so, they also need to run one on you. Maybe it's time for the truth about your conception to be revealed."

The startled look that settled over Jeremy's face revealed he was taking her speculation seriously.

"Do I share this now or do we confront your mother first?"

Jeremy rubbed the back of his neck while wondering aimlessly around the room. "Lucas is convinced I'm *your* half-brother. You think *I* could be his brother. That would make Herbert my biological father. Katie, do you understand the ramifications of such a revelation? Accusing a prominent bank president of such a crime would shake this entire city."

Katie leaned against the table. "Not fully, but I'm aware your folks will be added to the drama already playing out in our lives. Herbert will swear Jeannie seduced him. Whom will folks believe?"

"It'll be ugly regardless of what folks believe. And you don't think Lucas knows about his dad?"

"He has no clue. For sure, Herbert has to be one of the four. What will Lucas do if *he* turns out to be your brother?"

Jeremy clutched her shoulders. "Let's ask the chief to come back in."

After sharing everything, including Mrs. Webster's rape, the chief suggested they talk with Jeannie immediately. "Collecting DNA samples of felons is routine now. I'll need yours, Jeremy, and we need to find a way to get Herbert's. Let's do yours as well, Katie.

"I'd like for Jeannie and Doc to submit a report of that night. Katie, we're going to postpone the rest of your debriefing until tomorrow." As he held the door open for them, he added, "Lucas is unknowingly helping us solve an old crime."

Jeremy helped Katie climb into his truck and headed for his folks. "I want you and JD to go back home. Are you okay driving the truck?"

"I'm pregnant, Jeremy, not handicapped."

"I didn't mean to insinuate otherwise," he offered apologetically.

She smiled. "You're going to survive this pregnancy, Jeremy Webster."

"Let's hope we all survive the bombshell we are about to explode."

Doc and Jeannie had curious expressions on their faces when Katie and JD left Jeremy standing on their front porch … minus a vehicle. "Everything okay on the home front, Son?" Doc asked.

"I need to talk with you and Mom … alone."

Nineteen

After Jeremy explained everything, Jeannie confirmed what Katie had suspected. Herbert Taylor was one of the men who raped her. Katie's father was the other. "Your dad and I have felt for years that Lucas was your half-brother."

Jeremy was pacing. "Are you two willing to file a police report and tell the world what happened that night? I'll be okay with it."

"Lucas seems to be forcing the issue." Doc studied his son. "Now you know why we suggested you walk away from Katie five years ago. We judged the girl for the sins of her father and that was wrong."

He hugged the couple who had loved him in spite of his violent conception. "We've all made mistakes."

Jeannie wiped her tears. "How is Katie taking this?"

He rose and stared off into the mountains that surrounded them. "Better than I am at this point."

Doc grimaced. "Edgar was a shorter man and his eyes were a striking blue, like Katie's, but until the DNA results come back, there will be folks who insist your marriage to Katie is illegal. Are you prepared for that?"

"I can't lose my family ... not after all we've been through." He grabbed the phone and dialed the precinct. "Chief, please. This is urgent."

"Randolph here."

"Chief, will any of this have a bearing on our marriage until the DNA proves Herbert is my biological father?"

"Calm down, Jeremy. It will certainly give rise to suspicions, but nothing can or will be decided until DNA results come in. The tests will answer all questions. Aren't you glad we have that technology available?"

Jeremy breathed a sigh of relief. "I'm not giving up my family."

"Lucas' lawyer scheduled a press conference for ten o'clock this morning. Can't believe Herbert is permitting it."

"And you want me to believe I'm related to those two?"

The chief got quiet for a few seconds. "Actually, Jeremy, as I was talking to him today I studied the man with you in mind. I'm thinking of offering Katie a job on the force. Because of her, I think we will end up with charges against both of the Taylors before this is over."

"Talk about a reality check. My biological father raped my mother and my half-brother kidnapped my wife."

"Aren't you glad it's not all in the genes? Fifty percent good ones and the right environment served you well."

After Jeremy hung up, his dad drove him home. Katie met him at the door. "How'd it go?"

"Tough, but it's going to be okay." He kissed her and patted the baby. "How are you two doing?"

"He or she has been restless. I took a long shower in an effort to help us relax." She was rubbing her tummy. "I'll get your supper together while you clean up.

After showering and grabbing a bite to eat, Jeremy joined Katie in their bedroom. "Where is Ziggy?"

"In his doghouse on the back porch. He now includes Mrs. Carpenter in his patrol duties. Do you know she buys him a bone every week?"

Jeremy smiled. "She's a good neighbor. Maybe we need to consider leaving the gate between the properties open."

As they settled for the night, Jeremy confessed. "Mom confirmed it was Herbert Taylor and your dad who raped her."

Katie allowed another dark secret of her past to sink in. "Now I understand why my dad hated you so much. You were his conscience."

"Never thought of it that way." He pulled the cover over her legs. "You know some folks are going to claim our marriage isn't legal."

She turned enough to look in his face. "Jeremy, you and I know the truth. I don't care what the world thinks or says. We belong together."

"Then we agree."

Twenty

Jeremy was dressed when he kissed his sleeping wife the next morning. There was much to do before Lucas' distorted news hit the airwaves. A quick stop at the department to proceed with the DNA testing left him just enough time to arrive at the law office of an old football pal. He had called Jim late last night.

A friendly receptionist led him to a conference room. He was surprised, but pleased to see Jim's white partner present. After a brief time for catching up, they turned on the recorder and asked Jeremy to tell the story, starting with his mom's rape thirty years ago.

As the tale concluded, both men shook their heads. "Wow! That's as wild as a NYPD Blue segment. Count me in," Michael commented.

Jim spoke up. "Same here."

"The timing concerns me. Katie is less than three weeks from her due date," Jeremy said.

Michael looked at Jim. "I suggest we get her and JD out of the neighborhood for a few weeks." Michael placed a calming hand on Jeremy's arm. "Not far away, Friend. Just hidden from the public eye. This will stir a storm. I need to make a phone call."

Jeremy eased back down. "Don't take her far from the hospital."

"It's going to be okay, Sarge. In the meanwhile, we'll prepare a statement in response to Lucas' door opener. Have your parents call us. The sooner the better." Jim was gathering his notes and the tape from the recorder.

Michael put his hand on Jeremy's shoulder. "You are no stranger to the fall out of prejudice, but the heat is going higher than you dreamed possible. How supportive are your co-workers?"

"Pretty solid, I'd say."

"Good. It will probably be rough until we get the test results back."

Jeremy stopped on his way out the door. "It doesn't make any sense to me that Herbert would reveal Edgar's involvement to Lucas. What's on his mind?"

Jim grimaced. "Think about it, Jeremy. You are a living reminder of his evil deed."

"That's similar to the comment Katie made about her dad's hatred."

Jeremy headed home to help Katie and JD get ready for the trip downtown. The July temperatures were hanging around ninety instead of their usual mid-eighties. His enlarging wife had turned into a sweating machine. He shook his head thinking what a woman goes through to bring a baby into the world.

After sharing Jim and Michael's plans to place her and JD in a secluded place for a few weeks, he added, "I think I can persuade Mom and Dad to join you."

She scuffled out the door with her hand on her lower back. "Yeah, if your folks agree, I'm interested."

He was helping her into the passenger seat while JD crawled into his child restraint. "Need help buckling up, Son?"

"No, I can do it, Dad. Mom's the one who needs help."

"Careful, Son. Mom's a little sensitive these days."

"I believe you get smarter every day, Sergeant Webster," Katie volunteered.

They were in the precinct lobby when the Noon Show opened

with Lucas' lawyer making his announcement in front of the jail. "The accused kidnapper was actually on a mission of mercy to rescue a dear friend, Katie Williams, from an incestuous marriage to her half-brother, Jeremiah Daniel Webster. Katie and Jeremy have the same biological father."

Lucas' lawyer promised the rest of this revealing story would be forthcoming and asked that all charges against his client be dropped.

As the segment ended, Chief turned off the television and addressed the officers present. "You know better than most you can't believe everything you hear. DNA tests are in the works. In the meanwhile, Jeremy and his family need our support."

One of the deputies signaled for Jeremy. "There's a call from your lawyer on line two."

It was Jim. "Michael was able to gain access to a secluded farm located on the outskirts of Asheville. We want to move them now."

He gave Jeremy an address and instructions for getting them there tonight. By that evening, Katie and JD were sequestered on a lovely, isolated farm not far away. Doc and Jeannie followed with his big truck and trailer loaded with enough small engines to keep him busy for at least two weeks.

Jeremy stayed at home where a growing number of media vehicles and personnel were gathering. He, Ziggy and Mrs. Carpenter were holding down the home front. They agreed to open the gate between their back yards.

Katie called around 9:00 p.m. "Doc watches the drama unfolding on the television. Grammy and I are content to let it play out. Your folks are remarkable people, Jeremy. In spite of your beginnings, you are blessed."

"I couldn't have asked for better."

They talked a good hour and reluctantly said their goodnights. "I'm going to find a way to spend the night with you tomorrow, I promise."

About the time they hung up, Jim called. "Hey, we were able to secure a sample of Herbert Taylor's DNA today."

"How did …?"

"Don't ask. Paternity tests are the fastest and easiest. The chief has agreed to share his results if we will share this one. Your mom's story may break before the two weeks waiting period."

"You guys promise to watch out for her and Dad?" Jeremy asked.

"Scouts honor! I know this is hard on you and will get harder on your folks, but as lawyers, Michael and I are pleased to be part of it."

"I love it that our legal team is biracial, Michael."

"We did that on purpose and like the clients and cases it brings us."

Twenty-One

Two weeks later, Jeremy pulled out the note Valerie slipped into his hand when he worked a drunk driver accident earlier in the day.

> *Seems you made the wrong choice, Jeremy. That white girl of yours has been nothing but trouble, and now it turns out she is your sister. You know my number and address. When you get lonely, give me a call. I'm in a forgiving mood.*
>
> *Valerie*
>
> *Xoxoxo*

He threw it in the fire and spent the evening collecting the items Katie had requested and talking via phone to each of the secluded family members. Four days later Valerie intercepted him as he and another officer were leaving the ER. "I've been waiting to hear from you."

"In spite of the news reports, Valerie, I am happily married."

Her angry response gave insight into the bitterness his rejection had birthed. "I've asked your forgiveness. The rest is between you and God."

He and the officer walked away rather than continue a useless exchange. When they arrived back at headquarters, the chief called Jeremy into his office. "The DNA results are back."

The chief was quiet as Jeremy studied the summary report. "So Herbert Taylor *is* my biological father and Lucas is *my* half-brother."

"Yeah, and with this, we have enough evidence to file charges against Herbert for Jeannie's rape. His arrest is imminent."

Jeremy stared at the papers that verified those facts. "I know these refer to me, but I have no emotions connecting me with those two."

Chief Randolph flipped through the pages. "This settles the issue about your marriage, but has presented another quandary in the process. Jim and Michael want to see you in their office as soon as you can get there."

When Jeremy rose to leave, the chief added, "By the way, I've had several officers offer to cover your shifts when Katie goes into labor. Keep in touch."

He shook the hand of his boss and friend. "Thank you and them. I'll stop by Jim and Michael's before sharing this news with the folks and Katie."

Jim and Michael directed Jeremy into the conference room and closed the door. "You'd better sit down, Jeremy. We have some rather shocking news."

"I already know that Herbert Taylor is my biological dad and Lucas is my brother."

"There's more." They handed him another set of test results.

After reading the report, Jeremy glared at his lawyers. "Is this a joke?"

"Afraid not," Jim offered.

"You want me to believe that Katie and Lucas share the same biological mother?"

"That's what their DNA tests revealed."

Jeremy pushed back from the table. "How is that possible?"

"As Shakespeare would say, 'Something is rotten in Denmark.' Obviously there was more than one secret between Herbert and Edgar. The possibilities are intriguing."

"What am I going to tell Katie?" he asked as he stared out the window that overlooked the city.

"At the present time we don't see any connection between this and the case, but as wild as this whole story has been, we're not ruling that out. So unless or until it becomes pertinent, you wouldn't have to tell her, but somehow we think she deserves to know."

Michael was making some notes on his pad. "I'll have Rose's sample DNA by tomorrow afternoon." He looked up. "Don't ask."

"One other thought. Two other men out there know the truth about the night of your conception. We are going to challenge them to come forward after your mom's story goes public. If none do, then we are going to start digging."

Jeremy was in deep thought the entire drive to the farm. As he punched in the security code, he saw his dad's car approaching. When the gate swung open, he noticed Katie in the front seat.

Doc rolled down his window. "This wife of yours is in labor."

Stay calm, Webster. "Has the doctor been notified?"

Katie nodded as she grabbed her middle.

"Dad, let me lead." After turning around and pulling onto the highway, he contacted headquarters.

"Don't fret, Webster. We've got you covered." Not one traffic light was green and too many glances in his rearview mirror revealed Katie was having another contraction. When they finally arrived, Jeremy parked while Doc pulled into the emergency room entrance.

He tried to put on his professional calm as he opened Katie's door. "How close are the pains, Hon?"

"Under four minutes now. Your dad is a good coach. Did you know you were born at home?"

Jeremy looked at his dad. "How did you survive?"

At that moment, a smiling young man appeared with a wheelchair. "Your doctor alerted us that you were on the way, Mrs. Webster."

To Jeremy's relief, they by-passed the ER and took Katie straight to labor and delivery. That eliminated a possible run-in with Valerie.

For the next five hours, Jeremy experienced childbirth from a man's prospective. "I can't believe you went through JD's birth alone. Watching you hurts me. I can't imagine what it's like for you."

She held her breath as another pain hit. "These are the moments in life when wives have some less than kind thoughts and words for their husbands. I'm trying to be nice, but it just doesn't seem fair that men can't experience at least an hour or two of the birthing process." She stilled and groaned. "Get the nurse. I feel like I need to push."

When the doctor returned with the nurse, Jeremy moved to the head of the bed and watched in amazement as his daughter entered the world twenty minutes later. Her cry brought tears to his eyes.

After cleaning the new Webster arrival, the nurse allowed Jeremy a peek before placing the baby on Katie's chest. "You were awesome, Honey," he offered as he admired the two most beautiful women in the world. Love beyond anything he had imagined filled him at this moment. *Father, this must be a glimpse into Your love for us.*

In the midst of his joy, the harsh reality of his own birth intruded. He glanced between Katie and their child. What if this baby girl bore the seed of a man who had raped his wife? While a deeper love and respect for his parents took root, so did his first emotional response to Herbert Taylor. Pure hatred. The reaction alarmed him.

As Jeremy was dealing with the dichotomy of his emotions, so was his newly discovered brother. Lucas was hysterical. He alleged the tests were faulty or rigged.

While the brothers battled their personal internal wars, Herbert was arrested. Jeannie's rape and Jeremy's conception birthed a media blitz. Though Katie was protected from them at the hospital, Jeremy was not.

In spite of the hullabaloo that generated, Katie voiced her request. "Our marriage is no longer in question, Jeremy. Let's take our children home."

Jeremy was holding JD while Katie attended to Jaclyn. "Sounds wonderful to me. The first time these two are asleep simultaneously and you can keep your eyes open, we need to have a serious talk."

A knowing smile emerged. "That may be Christmas."

"Shows you how much I know about mommies and babies." He shifted JD to his back. "Come on, Son. Let's tell Grammy and Papa that Mama wants to go home."

Jeannie and Doc heeded Michael's advice to stay at the farm a while longer. Their story had stirred an explosion of controversy and the dust had not settled yet. Since Herbert's lawyer couldn't deny Jeremy's parentage, he was painting Jeannie as the seducer of white men. Herbert and Lucas were soon out on bail. The fury and hatred they tried to incite must have make Lucifer smile.

It took the day to get his family settled back at home. When both children were sleeping, he pulled Katie onto his lap. "I miss the rounded effect," he said as he patted her tummy.

She punched him. "Mind your tongue, Mister. The hormones haven't settled yet." She placed her hand over his. "Now the challenge of getting these extra pounds off and getting back in shape. Believe it or not, breast feeding helps."

He rubbed her arm. "Did you nurse JD?"

"Yeah, I did. Aunt Bea convinced me it would be the best for both of us."

Jeremy lightly kissed her. "Thank you." His tone sobered. "I have some news to share with you."

"You make it sound so serious."

"It is, so maybe sitting in my lap wasn't such a good idea."

She inched onto the space beside him. "Now I'm curious. Business or personal?"

"It's about your DNA results."

She straightened. "Mine? I thought the tests confirmed that you and Lucas are kin folks."

"They did, but yours also held a surprise."

"Mine?" she questioned as she scooted to the edge of the seat.

Jeremy couldn't figure out a way to soften the blow. "Honey, you are also related to Lucas."

Her right pointer aimed for her chest while her eyebrows met in the middle. "Me?"

"Yeah. As crazy as it sounds, the tests revealed that you and Lucas have the same mother."

She waved him off. "That … is absurd."

"The tests prove otherwise."

Katie faced him with stormy eyes. "Then how do you explain Martha and Rose? And who else knows about this convoluted revelation?"

He rose and gently put his hands on her shoulders. "Only the chief, Michael and Jim. There are three possibilities, Katie. Your mom, Rose Taylor or a third, unknown woman. Did your folks ever hint of adoption?"

Her head shook from side to side more than once. "Never."

Jeremy studied his attractive wife. "Did you ever see photos of your mom when she was pregnant?"

"Come to think of it … no."

"Did folks ever suggest you favored either of your parents?"

"Dad used to tell me I reminded him of pictures of his mom when she was young. I'm nothing like Mama. Do you think it's Rose?"

He hugged her. "I don't see any resemblance there either. I'm leaning towards the third option." Jeremy wrapped a curl around his finger. "The only thing I can see that you and Lucas have in common is your hair and that didn't come from Martha or Rose."

Katie was beside herself. "Don't you think it's a little unbelievable that both of us are related to Lucas?"

"A little? Jim and Michael are still in a daze. Except for the fact that DNA tests don't lie, none of us would even consider such a possibility."

Katie leaned back in the chair and closed her eyes. "I'm hoping I'm in the middle of a nightmare and you're going to wake me soon."

Jeremy knelt by her chair. "This nightmare is real, Katie."

Opening her eyes and touching his cheek with her fingers, she summarized their situation. "My brother kidnapped me to save me from his brother. Bizarre doesn't even come close to describing our lives at this moment."

"Obviously the Taylor and Williams families shared more than one dark secret, Honey. Michael and Jim said we need to keep this quiet for a while."

"Yeah, that's so folks won't put us all on a space ship and send us to another planet."

Twenty-Two

By the middle of September, Jim and Michael had DNA proof Rose was not the answer to the mom mystery. That left Martha or a third party. Katie offered a hairbrush retrieved from an old travel case in the attic.

She wondered what Aunt Edith knew but wasn't willing to risk such a conversation. Isaac was an old family friend. Would he know? Maybe, but she decided to approach Jeannie and Doc first.

The noise coming from the in-law efficiency reminded her Jeremy's folks were moving in today. Jim and Michael's idea. Katie wished it could be permanent.

She joined JD and Ziggy. "Watch, Mom. He fetches my ball every time now." She watched until she heard someone open the passage door into the hearth room.

"Anything I can help you with before you go?" Jeannie asked as she made her way to Jaclyn.

"Yeah, I need to talk with you." After slipping her feet into her shoes, Katie settled on the sofa. "Were you surprised when Jeremy told you about me and Lucas being related?"

Jeannie and baby Jaclyn relaxed in the chair opposite Katie. "At first, but Doc made a point. If two young men would plan and rape the same woman in each other's presence, they could just as easily be involved in wife-swapping or sharing the same mistress."

Katie's eyes revealed her shock. "Both were in the room with you the entire time?"

"Katie, you have to understand the mind-set of racism. It sees us as inferior beings. They also made my husband and four-year-old son stay in the room. That's why I didn't resist them." Tears filled Jeannie's eyes.

"That's why James was furious when Jeremy married you. Your godly husband reminded him of a powerful truth ... *Although the sins of your father have impacted your life, they were not your sins.*"

Katie stared at her mother-in-law. "How can you and Doc ... or even Jeremy, for that matter ... love and accept me as part of your family, Jeannie?"

Gentle black arms embraced the child of her abuser. "For years Doc and I couldn't, Katie. Like James, we had projected the sins of your father on you ... his innocent daughter. Jeremy helped us see how wrong we had been.

"That revelation opened our eyes to the blame game where the sins of the guilty are attributed to the innocent. Your love for Jeremy unearthed that lie."

More tears than words characterized the next fifteen minutes of conversation. A quick look at her watch reminded Katie of her appointment. "JD is in the backyard with Ziggy. I'll take Jaclyn with me. Maybe we can talk more this evening."

After Katie's final check-up with her gynecologist, she dropped by the funeral home. Isaac was with a family at the time, so she slipped into the ladies' room to change Jaclyn. By the time they finished, Isaac was free.

"Katie Webster, introduce me to the newest family member."

After catching up, Katie pointed to a small room off the lobby area. "Isaac, could we talk privately?"

He reached for the baby carrier. "Sure. Did the will and probate go smoothly?"

"Yeah, everything was in order. This is a different matter."

"Okay," he answered as he placed Jaclyn near her mother.

"How well did you know my parents and the Taylors before I was born?"

"Grew up with them." He stroked his chin a few times before continuing. "Edgar and Herbert were thicker than thieves growing up. Their adventures bordered on the wild side."

"Were you shocked to learn that they had raped Jeannie Webster?"

His eyes apologized for his answer. "Yes, but I didn't find it unbelievable. Rose and Martha gave them a respectable standing in the community, but both men were womanizers. Add a lifetime of engrained racial prejudice passed down from their folks, and I can see them justifying their actions."

Shame filled her heart. "What about swapping wives or sharing a mistress?"

"Now Katie, those are some pretty serious accusations."

"Isaac, Lucas and I have the same mother, and Rose has been ruled out. So either Martha birthed us or they shared a mistress."

He placed a gentle hand on her arm. "Katie, neither woman was ever pregnant."

The deeper she dug, the greater the shock and disgust … and shame. "Are you suggesting Edgar might not be my birth father?"

Isaac pushed up his sleeve to check the time. "I personally think he is. You favor his mother."

Isaac rose and paced before turning to face her. "Years ago a story circulated about a beautiful, young girl who worked at the Grove Park Inn. Never met her personally, but reports said she had movie star looks. Seems some rich men convinced her she could make more money selling her body than cleaning rooms. Heard Herbert was one of her customers. Could be your dad knew her as well, but birthing babies? Never heard about that."

"Did you hear a name associated with her?"

"Never did."

My father was a whoremonger and my mother was a prostitute? "I feel sick, Isaac."

He patted her arm. "Not only are you not responsible for the sins of your parents, Katie, the generational curse or bent toward the same sins can end with you and Jeremy."

Katie's eyes enlarged. "What is a generational curse or bent?"

Isaac glanced at the sleeping baby. "Just as this child carries the physical genes of her parents and grandparents, so she will be influenced by her spiritual heritage … the good and the evil. Think about the struggles, lifestyles or beliefs of parents that you also see in their children. There's more than environmental influences involved, Katie."

Katie studied Jaclyn. "Is prejudice a generational curse or bent?"

"Prejudice is taught and caught. A few years ago, a Bible scholar by the name of Derek Prince wrote a book on blessings and curses. I'll loan you my copy." He excused himself.

When he returned with the book, Katie was pondering their conversation. "Though you've shared some ugly truth about my background today, Isaac, you've given me hope."

"Katie, you and Jeremy are reaping the harvest of other folks' evil. For the sake of your children and their children, forgive your parents … completely. Then sow God's love and forgiveness towards those who see you as targets of their hatred and ignorance today. You can leave your children a legacy of blessings. Life is hard enough without the weight of past generations."

Tears clouded her vision. "Thank you for making time for me today."

He placed a fatherly arm around her shoulders. "My parents left me at the door of the Good Shepherd Children's Home when I was two-years-old, Katie. Our stories are different, but I understand some of your pain."

A smile broke through her tears. "I knew you were a kindred spirit." She scrunched her shoulders to wipe her eyes on Jaclyn's burp cloth. "Where does Aunt Edith fit into all of this?"

"Edith and Edgar were always more than friends. She was shocked and furious when he married Martha."

Katie's eyes expressed the shock of yet another secret. "Holy

Moly, Edith and Dad? That explains a lot." Afraid to ask but needing to know, she dug deeper. "Could she be my birth mother?"

"No. She was never pregnant. I'm guessing there is a third party involved."

Another dark secret?

As she and Grammy were setting the table that evening, she questioned Jeannie. "Was Mom ever pregnant?"

Jeannie kept her focus on the transfer of chicken and dumplings to a serving bowl. "No, Honey. Folks figured one of Edgar's women was your mother."

"Folks knew my birth mother was a woman of the streets?" Tears were filling her eyes.

Jeremy rushed to her side. "Honey, my biological father is a rapist and bigot. We may bear some of their genes, but we are not them. We can't allow our parents' past to determine who we are today." He smiled at his daughter who was rooting around on his chest. "This little lady thinks you're pretty special."

Katie reached for her hungry daughter. "You ever heard of generational blessings and curses?"

"Some, but not enough to understand the ramifications of it all. Why?" He followed her to the rocking chair in the hearth room.

"Isaac mentioned it today. He gave me a book to read."

"Maybe we need to read it together."

"I agree. Eat without me. I'll join you when her tummy is full."

Jeremy kissed her on the cheek and left. She replayed her conversation with Isaac as she considered the child at her breast.

Katie joined the family after placing a sleeping Jaclyn in the large rocking cradle Doc had made. "Best chicken and dumplings ever, Mom," Jeremy said while removing any evidence from his face and then patting his stomach.

"Yeah, can I have more?" JD asked as he lifted his plate.

"May I," Katie corrected.

"Grammy, you know what I mean when I use *can*, don't you?"

"Eat your dumplings, Child."

Conversation was light that evening until the youngest dumpling lover called it a night. That's when Katie shared her conversation with Isaac. "How much do you two know about Dad's involvement with women?"

They looked at each other and lowered their heads before answering. "It doesn't seem fitting to tell you any of that, Katie."

"And this is the man who disowned me?" Disgust and shame shaded her face.

When Jeannie scooted close, the men headed to the porch. "Hatred and guilt can breed some mighty cruel and unreasonable behavior, Katie. Remember what he knew about Jeremy."

Katie's head was in her hands.

"Yours and Jeremy's pasts sure are a tangle of webs, Child, but God is not surprised or ashamed to call you … His." She hugged Katie and then joined the men,

"Son, Katie needs lots of tender love and care right now. Finding out all this and having a new baby ... be gentle with her." Doc and Jeannie dismissed themselves for the night.

Jeremy found his wife staring at the empty fireplace. "There's a romantic moon outside. Will you join me?"

She accepted the offered hand.

"Rough day?" Jeremy asked as he led her to the wicker love seat on the porch.

"Only when I think about the past. My present life fills me with more joy and gratitude than I can hold in, Jeremy."

They snuggled quietly for a long time … listening to the audible evidence of life around them and gazing at the vastness of the world above them.

"Do you ever contemplate the mystery and secrets of the darkness, Jeremy?"

He hugged her close. "That's a rather philosophical question, Honey."

"It's been that kind of day." He listened.

"Everything I've learned makes me love and appreciate you and us more, Jeremy. We are blessed in spite of our messy past." She leaned in for an intimate kiss.

"I noticed a big red heart around today's date. Any significance?" Jeremy asked.

A playful smile emerged. "As a matter of fact, there is." She wiggled out of his arms and headed for their suite. Jeremy followed. When he heard the bathroom lock click, he smiled.

"Is this one of those surprise pit stops?" he softly inquired.

"You have a good memory, Mr. Webster."

Twenty-Three

Life settled into a pleasant routine as the weeks passed. Doc and Jeannie moved back home. Jaclyn was a growing, happy baby. JD was thrilled to be in kindergarten. Katie and Jeremy were adjusting to the demands of and enjoying the blessings of two children.

Jeremy was concerned about Katie's occasional brooding spells. Was it post-partum? Lingering questions about her past? Or both?

It was October 3. JD was already in bed and Katie was changing Jaclyn's diaper when Jeremy made it home. He kissed the back of Katie's neck and tickled his daughter's toes. "How are my girls?"

His daughter's head turned in the direction of the familiar voice and rewarded him with a smile and air-attacking feet. "She's a heart stealer, Honey." Waiting until Katie had Jaclyn's sleeper snapped, he picked up the youngest family member and shared a special father-daughter time before dropping by JD's room.

After feeding Jaclyn, Katie found Jeremy watching the UT and Ole Miss game.

"Peyton's having a great night. Looks like we'll stay in the top ten again this week," Jeremy informed her between bites.

"Don't you find it interesting that Dad admired your athletic abilities and followed all your high school and college games, yet had no respect for you as a human being? What kind of sense does that make?"

"Prejudice not only infects the heart, Honey; it also warps the mind."

They watched the game until half time. "Let's get these dishes cleaned up before that growing girl demands your attention again." Jeremy studied her. "I've been watching you. Something's brewing."

She began wiping the countertops. "What would you say to a trip to Roanoke the next time you get off?"

"Roanoke?"

"Yeah, I want to run a DNA test on Aunt Bea. Think that's doable?"

Jeremy backed up to a barstool. "You think she might be your birth mom?"

Katie's eyes lit up. "Been giving it some consideration, and the more I think about it, the more I think it's possible."

"But Katie, she's a godly woman."

"Doesn't mean she always was, now does it?"

He handed her the last item to put in the dishwasher. "How are you going to handle our visit?"

"We could use our anniversary as an excuse to get away ... though we have to take the children. Romantic thought, isn't it? She'd be thrilled to see JD, and I do want her to meet Jaclyn."

He grinned. "If you and Little Bit weren't so attached, I'd suggest revisiting the Love Nest. Next year, Lord willing."

Early Friday morning, October 25, the Jeremy Webster family set out for Roanoke. It was an Isaiah 55:12 day. One could almost hear the mountains and hills celebrating God's autumn extravaganza. Brilliantly painted leaves floated and swirled through the air to join the multitudes that had already blanketed the forest floor.

Katie voiced her thoughts. "Can you hear creation praising its Creator this morning, Jeremy?"

"Inspiring isn't it? I never found a spot that connects with my spirit and points me to God quite like this one."

"The peaks, like praise, lift our eyes above the mundane and point to the Almighty." Katie offered as she checked on their wide-eyed five-year-old and slumbering three-month-old.

As the trip progressed, JD began recalling memories of Aunt Bea. When his conversation died down, Katie persuaded him to color in his big truck book. "I'll make one for Aunt Bea, Mom."

Jaclyn woke hungry and wet. Lunch at the Cracker Barrel solved those problems and the general hunger factor as well. "Their chicken and dumplings are almost as good as Grammy's," JD offered as they exited the family restaurant.

JD roused from a nap as they neared Aunt Bea's subdivision. His internal GPS kicked in. "I remember this place. Turn at that blue house, Daddy. We lived in the brick one at the end of the street."

By the time Jeremy turned in, JD was unbuckled and opening his door. "Aunt Bea has company." He checked out the beautifully restored old pickup truck in her driveway before knocking on the door. He wasn't tall enough to reach the buzzer.

Katie heard his exclamation before she recognized the person. "Kyle!"

The startled man looked at JD and then the vehicle. Recovering quickly, he swept his little friend in his arms. "Little Buddy, I wasn't sure I'd ever see you again."

"I have a baby sister now. Her name is Jaclyn, but I call her Jackie." Oblivious to the pain that bit of news was to his friend, JD was urging his family to hurry.

Aunt Bea joined Kyle. "Landsakes, look who's here." She opened her arms and JD responded.

The two adults in the vehicle were just as stunned as Kyle and Aunt Bea. "Jeremy, what should we do?"

He was already getting out of the car and reaching for the baby carrier. "Go see your old friends … unless you have a better idea."

She reached for the diaper bag. "So much for surprising Aunt Bea."

As they walked towards the house, Kyle and JD went inside. Aunt

Bea stayed on the porch. After hugging Katie and shaking Jeremy's hand, she stared at the newest family member. "Oh, my goodness, this baby girl is her mama made over with a permanent sun tan." She looked between Jeremy and Katie. "Will she come to me?"

When Jeremy lifted his daughter out of the carrier and placed her in Bertha's arms, two crocodile tears rolled down her cheeks. "Aren't you the alert one?" She nodded towards the door. "Go on in, folks."

When they entered, JD grabbed Kyle's hand. "Come see my sister. She's too little to play with me, but she's growing fast."

Kyle looked at the baby in Bertha's arms and then at Katie. "She's beautiful … like her mother, JD."

"Yeah, that's what Daddy says."

As the men's eyes met, Jeremy extended his hand. "Is that your truck in the driveway?"

"Just bought it last week. Never owned one before."

Jeremy chuckled under his breath. "You know what they say. A man and his truck are the modern version of a man and his horse."

"Never owned a horse either." Kyle's uncomfortableness was palatable. "Say, I'm going next door so you folks can visit."

JD tugged on his pants leg. "We just got here."

Kyle knelt in front of the lad. "Tell you what. I'll be next door for a while before heading out. You come see me, okay?"

JD looked at Jeremy. "Can I go now, Daddy?"

Jeremy tousled the boy's curly hair. "Sure. Go on."

A softening washed over Kyle's face as he lifted JD into his arms. "I'll send him back when I head out."

When Kyle left, Katie breathed a sigh of relief. "Aunt Bea, surely he doesn't live in our old place?"

"Live there? No. Rent it? Yes. It's become his get-away. He and his folks have had some rough days. He tried to live in the house he bought for you but eventually sold it. He still has his apartment close to work, but he ends up here a couple of evenings a week. Sometimes he spends the night and other times just a few hours."

"I thought he was moving away."

"He's opened a business in Denver and has been traveling back and forth, but plans to move there permanently by the end of the year."

Aunt Bea situated Jaclyn so she could see her family. "Getting to know Kyle has given me a window into the woes of the wealthy. I better understand Solomon's statement … *the rich seldom get a good night's sleep.*"

Jaclyn became restless. "Why don't you and Jeremy make a visit to the China Lantern while I feed this one?"

Aunt Bea grabbed a sweater on her way out. "Come on, Son. I'll show you where to buy the best Chinese food between here and Hong Kong."

JD stayed with Kyle. By the time Jeremy and Aunt Bea returned, Katie had the baby asleep. "Jeremy, will you go next door and get JD. Invite Kyle to join us." She and Bertha began setting the table.

As they were bustling around, Katie began the conversation she came to have. "Aunt Bea, you said you knew my folks before I came to live here. When was that?"

Bertha stooped to retrieve the dropped fork. "Our paths had crossed years earlier and we managed to stay in touch."

Katie stopped all action to watch Bea's body language. "How and where did you meet them?"

A stoic look overtook Bea's face as she straightened to face her interrogator. "Why are you asking?"

Katie didn't blink. "I found out recently that Martha wasn't my biological mother. Now I'm wondering if Edgar was my father."

"They never told you?"

A sternness took over Katie's countenance. "Told me what, Aunt Bea? It's rather disturbing to be twenty-five and discover you are not who you thought you were."

Bea softened. "What do you want from me, Katie?"

"I've been wondering how much you know about my past." She waited quietly as Bea withdrew the food packets from the large sack and began placing them on the table.

As she folded the bags, her eyes focused on Katie. "Years ago, I worked in Asheville. I met your dad through a mutual friend."

Katie's heart rate doubled. "Was this mutual friend, Herbert Taylor?"

Bea's body froze. "Yes, how did you find out?"

Katie grabbed the back of the closest chair and took a deep breath as another dark secret surfaced. "It's a long story. Did Mama know about you and Daddy?"

"She knew." Bea hung her head as tears began pushing passed her eyelids.

"Is Edgar my father?" Katie was shaking.

"Your father is dead and your mother was a person you don't need to know about. Let's stick to the Aunt Bea relationship, okay?"

She turned away from Katie. "Jeremy, JD, it's time to eat. Never did like cold Chinese food."

Katie was still staring at Bea as Jeremy and JD took their seats. Her husband did his best to ease the tension with lighter conversation, but it was JD who introduced another topic.

"Mama, Kyle is sad we went away. Can he come live with us?"

Adult eyes widened and mouths dropped. Katie answered. "Honey, Kyle needs to find his own family."

"Can we pray for God to help him find one?"

"Good idea, Son," Jeremy answered.

They made it through the rest of the meal and a strained farewell. As they were pulling into the street, Jeremy pointed to the diaper bag. "We'll soon have proof of your suspicions, Katie, but then what?"

"The test is not necessary, Jeremy, but let's follow through anyway." She looked out the window at some of the familiar scenes of her past. "All the time I lived here she knew who I was. I didn't have a clue."

"How could you? Except for the hair there is no resemblance."

"What about Lucas?"

Twenty-Four

It was late Monday evening, December 2, 1996. Katie was staring at the test results that confirmed Bertha was her mother. JD was in bed. Jaclyn was playing on a pad to the side of the fireplace.

"Jeremy, talk to Jim and Michael about sharing this info with Lucas." She was scanning the report. "Beats me why Bea isn't willing to talk about it." Solemn eyes waited to catch her husband's full attention. "Our family trees would give genealogy buffs a permanent migraine."

"Yeah, but what a potential showcase for the grace of God! Ever studied Jesus' genealogy? He has three. The gospel of John records his heavenly lineage. Matthew records his adoptive father's family tree and Luke offers his human bloodlines through Mary. You'll find some folks of questionable character in his earthly lines."

A slight smile replaced a troubled expression. "You're telling me there's a reason for all those challenging names?"

"Bible scholars say so. That gives me hope for us, Katie."

"Hmmm." Maybe this was a good time to throw out a reoccurring thought. "Speaking of kinfolks, do you think we could get Lucas' sentence lessened?"

Jeremy straightened up to get a better glimpse of her face. "Are you serious?"

"He's our brother, Jeremy."

The bewildered look on her husband's face made Katie laugh. "Does it sound that crazy?"

"Yes, but grace usually does."

Jeremy's focus shifted. "Look, Katie, Jaclyn is on all fours." She was rocking back and forth and then splattering on her tummy … only to start the routine over again. "Watching her is filling in some of the missing years with JD." He picked up the bundle of energy that was as enamored with him as he was with her.

"I'll talk to Jim and Michael about your thoughts regarding Lucas."

"Thank you."

January and February flew by and except for JD's birthday, life was routine and uneventful. Still no word from Bea. Lucas' lawyer, who now possessed a copy of the DNA results, requested a meeting between Lucas and Katie. It was set for March 18.

Jeannie had dropped in to stay with the children. "How are you and Doc holding up with all the stir over Herbert's trial?"

"Life is filled with troubles, but God is faithful, Katie."

"How about James?"

"It's been harder for him. He has struggled with more than skin color since that night. I think he's afraid to marry. You've helped him see it's the heart, not the skin that determines one's behavior. Now if he can get over the other emotional wounds of that life altering event."

Tears came to Katie's eyes. "I can't imagine what something like that does to a child." She glanced at her watch. "I'd better run. When Jaclyn wakes, you can give her juice and teething biscuits. I'll be back as soon as I can."

Katie was five minutes early for their meeting. Robert Cunningham showed up first. After both were seated, he opened his briefcase and pulled out a file. "Katie, as Lucas' lawyer, I appreciate what you've tried to do on his behalf. I think it's beginning to sink in to him as well."

She was tracing the woodgrain pattern on the table. "The fact that pesky Lucas is my brother is growing on me." She lifted her head and smiled. "Friends with brothers tell me that's a good sign."

Mr. Cunningham laughed. "I think my sisters would agree."

The door opened and Lucas walked in. The dynamics between them had changed.

"Why don't you sit there, Lucas?" Mr. Cunningham pointed to the chair opposite Katie.

Lucas' eyes didn't veer from Katie as he lowered his body into the chair. "Can you believe the mess our folks made of our lives?"

His acceptance of the facts helped Katie relax some. "I'm betting we qualify for the Guinness Book of Records."

"How did you figure it out?" He was studying her physical features differently this time.

She smiled as memories surfaced. "Remember the kidnapping episode?"

"I'd rather not, but yes ... at least until I took that sleeping powder."

Lucas listened intently as she shared how the puzzle pieces came together. "I know our biological mother."

He gasped. "You do?"

"Yeah, she was my landlady and neighbor those five years I lived in Roanoke?"

His eyes widened. "Are you kidding me?"

"Nope. I had no idea."

He looked at her with the strangest expression. "Katie, I used to be proud to be Herbert Taylor's son, but now I'm ashamed of who I am, aren't you?"

"It's true we have a lot of past baggage to deal with, but it doesn't have to define us. I'm blessed with a loving husband, two beautiful children and caring in-laws. I'm offering you a place in our family, but that means you have to choose to see us through God's eyes of love and acceptance instead of the eyes of prejudice and ignorant men."

He leaned back in his chair. "Mom and Dad aren't happy about any of this."

"Deception is a cruel companion, Lucas. And if repentance doesn't accompany its exposure to truth, then the fingers will point outward. You now know the truth and like them, you have to make a choice."

"I'm facing prison, Katie. Will you still want me in your life when that happens?"

"Yes, and when you get out, we'll be waiting for you."

Eyes so like Jeremy's studied her. "How do I see Jeremy as my brother instead of a black man?"

She reached across the table for his hand. "He's not one or the other, Lucas. He's both. He is your black brother. Close your eyes."

He hesitated.

She patted his hand. "Come on, close your eyes."

"Pretend there are twenty other folks in this room and ten of them are of a different race. "Would it make a difference to you if you were blind?"

"I guess it wouldn't."

"How would you decide whom you liked and whom you didn't?"

He opened his eyes. "How they treated each other and me?"

"Exactly. So maybe you need to wear a blindfold for a few months so that truth will become embedded deep enough to root out all the lies you've believed. The blessing of a truth transplant is that it clears up the vision. God's rainbow of skin colors is a thing of beauty. I can't imagine Jeremy or our children white."

A tear slipped out of Lucas' probing eyes. "I can't believe you care about me after all I've done to you and Jeremy."

"Jeremy and his folks taught me the importance of forgiveness, Lucas. That and choosing to love folks who judge us is not easy, but it is freeing and healthy. Makes life a lot sweeter too."

Slowly he eased out of his chair and made his way around the table. She pushed back and stood within arms' length of the man who tried to kidnap her.

"So what's it going to be, Brother?"

He awkwardly reached for a hand. Katie wrapped her arms around his waist and wept. Lucas slowly lowered his chin on her head. "I've always loved you, Katie. Now I know why."

She stepped away and punched him ... hard. "You have to promise to quit being a pest."

His smile gave way to concern. "I'll work on it. What do I tell my folks?"

"The truth. I'm guessing you'll need help setting up some healthy boundaries where they are concerned. In the meanwhile, move out and live your own life. Become a man of character. Admit what you've done and accept the consequences. Give some serious consideration to God. Hopefully, by the time you get out, you'll know who God is and who He declares you to be."

This time he hugged her warmly. "Thanks, Katie."

"Give Jeremy a chance, will you?"

"It's going to take time, but I promise to think about that blindfold and truth transplant theory of yours."

Twenty-Five

Katie and Jeremy's plea of leniency came as a surprise to some folks, including the judge. May 15, 1997, Lucas' trial concluded. "Lucas Taylor, if your brother and sister hadn't pleaded for mercy on your behalf, I'd have given you the maximum allowed by law. These are unusual circumstances, so I'm going to sentence you to two years in prison and one year of probation. Your brother has agreed to house you in their efficiency that year. One word from him and I'll stick you back in jail to finish out your term. Understood?"

"Yes, Sir. Thank you."

"Thank them."

Before they took him away, a humbled man did just that. The siblings parted with a promise to visit.

By the time Jaclyn's July birthday rolled around, she was walking. "How many of these do you think we can handle, Katie?" Jeremy asked as he played in the floor with both children.

She threw a pillow at him, which he tossed back playfully. "Did you hear that Herbert's lawyers got another six months delay?"

"Other than that, things are unusually quiet, aren't they?" Katie picked up the basket of clothes she had been folding.

"Yeah, and quiet is wonderful."

Jeremy helped JD with his bath while Katie finished the laundry and took care of Jaclyn. The toddler was asleep before Jeremy made it to her room. "She plays hard. I love the fact that she sleeps all night now."

They tiptoed out of the room and visited with JD until his bedtime. "Wait a minute, Dad." JD prayed his simple prayer and ended with his usual requests. A family for Kyle and a baby brother for him and Jackie. "Night, Mom. Night, Dad."

"Good night, Sweet Boy."

"I'll help with the kitchen," Jeremy offered. He sidestepped to grab the ringing phone.

"Hi, Aunt Bea." He motioned for Katie. "Yeah, she's close by. Just a second."

"Hello," Katie said as she angled the phone on her shoulder so both could hear.

"Alright, Katie. I know you've been praying for me, because I've been miserable. So here's the deal. Yes, I am your biological mother and Edgar was your biological father. I am also Lucas' biological mom and Herbert is his biological father. Sadly, Martha and Rose knew those facts."

Katie breathed a sigh of relief. "I have DNA to prove all of that except the part about Edgar being my father."

Katie heard the woman take a deep breath. "The rest is too ugly to dig up." There was a long pause. "I'd like to be a part of your lives … if you can forgive me for my part in the wounds of your past."

Katie struggled to control her voice and choose her words. "I wouldn't be here if not for you, so I guess we need to go from there. What's next?"

A repentant voice asked with quiet boldness. "Can we start over?"

"We can try. We have a small efficiency connected to the house. Why don't you come visit for a week or two?"

Katie heard the sniffles on the other end. "I'll see what I can do." She cleared her throat. "Katie, I learned to love you and JD those years you lived here. I'd have taken care of you if Edgar hadn't given me a penny." Silence followed and Katie waited. "Do you think Lucas will give me a chance?"

"I'll send you his address. Herbert and Rose have disowned him now that he's in prison. Maybe knowing you care will help."

"I'll let you know when I can come for a visit. Oh, by the way, Kyle phoned the other day. I think the man is in love. Some girl he met in Denver. He sounded happy."

"JD will be glad to hear that good news. Thanks for calling."

There was a lightness in her voice. "Well, it was that ... or give up sleeping. Talk to you soon."

Jeremy took the phone from her hand and put it back in its rack. "It's a start, Katie."

"I know. I've gone from being disowned and having no one except JD to having a husband and another child ... and now a brother and a mother. It's a little mind-boggling."

"Honey, aren't you glad God specializes in messes?"

She chucked as she wiped more tears. "He's had His hands full with ours."

Twenty-Six

Bea arrived two weeks before JD's school opened. It was a week of tears and healing. Lucas called while she was there. "Will you visit? If it weren't for Katie and Jeremy, I'd have no one."

"I'll come." She handed the phone back to Katie.

"Whatever and whoever she used to be … she's not anymore."

"Come soon, Katie. It's rough in here."

"We'll see what we can do, Lucas."

Katie set up visitation for September 14. Bertha met her at the prison. After the security clearance, they waited in a room that was becoming a part of Katie's life. The door opened and prisoners began to file through one at a time. The minute Lucas smiled at Katie; Bea's hand flew to her mouth. "Except for the hair, he is Herbert Taylor twenty-five years ago."

His steps slowed when his gaze shifted to his mother. Only the Lord knew what was going through his mind at that moment. Slowly his attention shifted back to Katie. "Thanks for coming." He took his seat on the opposite side of the table.

Bea had become a tear factory.

"Why the tears?" Lucas' voice had an edge to it.

She reached for a tissue. "I never thought I'd ever see you again."

Questioning eyes searched hers. "What kind of woman were you?"

Bea reached for several tissues. "One of the worst sort, Lucas."

"Don't you think Katie and I have a right to know?" His green lasers penetrated her will.

Working hard to maintain control, Bea spilled her story. "Lucas, I was a young girl when I moved to Asheville to work at the Grove Park Inn. One day a middle-aged man offered me more money than I'd seen in my life in exchange for my time after work the three days a month he was in town. My father had robbed me of my innocence years earlier. Being paid well for something that had no meaning or value to me seemed a fair exchange. Since he only came three days a month, I began to pick up other clients. Before long, I quit working as a maid and rented a nice house close by. Some of the local men began calling for appointments. Your dad became a regular.

"One day Herbert handed me a blank check and told me to fill in the numbers. He needed an heir and Rose wasn't cooperating. He wanted exclusive rights to my body until I could give him a baby. I put a ridiculous number on the check. You were born a year later. To Rose's horror, he presented you to her three days after you were born."

"No wonder she's always resented me." Lucas' eyes filled with disgust. "You were worse than a prostitute."

Bea hung her head and nodded.

Katie had listened in utter dismay. "How did Edgar get involved?"

"Oh, Herbert always was one to brag. One year after Lucas was born, Edgar approached me with the same proposition. Martha was barren. When I told him how much Herbert had paid, he handed me a blank, signed check." Her chin trembled. "You were born fourteen months later."

Bea's eyes took on a faraway look. "It's hard to explain what happens to a woman's mind and heart when she uses her body for her livelihood. I had no emotional attachment to the men in my life or the babies that grew in my body."

"Were we the only two?" Katie asked.

"Yes."

Moisture gathered in Katie's eyes. "Now I know why I always felt detached ... until I met Jeremy." She looked at Lucas. "We were the products of an immoral business deal, Lucas."

A resolute daughter faced her mother. "Why did you decide to tell the truth now?"

"Pastor Joel taught a lesson recently on generational blessings and curses. I knew then that you needed to know the truth," a remorseful woman responded.

Lucas reached for Katie's hand. "We share a shameful legacy, Sis."

He zeroed in on Bea. "Love has always been an elusive pursuit in my life. And I'm numb where you are concerned, but Katie is winning my heart. I'm even adjusting to having a black brother. They have risen above the depravity of their past. I'm trying to find my way."

Bea hugged Lucas and walked to the back of the room.

"I'm glad I knew her as Aunt Bea before hearing that story," Katie offered. "And Lucas, her past doesn't determine our future."

"At least she's sorry and admits she did wrong. I don't see any remorse in my dad, Katie. Hatred seems to be part of who he is."

"Makes one wonder what his story entails, Lucas. I would never have known about God's love apart from Jeremy and Bea."

I met two inmates recently who have been sharing their stories about this God you talk about."

The guard announced the time was up. "Are you going to be okay?" Katie asked.

"Actually, I feel better. How about you?"

"As hard as it was to hear, it brings clarity to our past and offers understanding of some lingering struggles. Can't believe Aunt Bea and our mother are one and the same person."

They shared a warm hug before he was escorted out.

Katie and Bea were quiet as they went through the exiting processes. Katie voiced one of her thoughts as they neared their vehicles. "For now, I'm going to keep calling you Aunt Bea."

Bea nodded and wept.

Jeremy listened much and said little that night. Katie fell asleep from emotional exhaustion.

Twenty-Seven

A year passed, Except for two more delays for Herbert's trial, life was pleasant, fulfilling and very busy.

As the end of October neared, they managed a return trip to *the Love Nest* to celebrate their third anniversary. By the time the scenic trip back home ended, both were ready to tackle the blessed challenges of caring for their offspring.

The next four weeks passed quickly. Thanksgiving came and the Websters enjoyed another family reunion. Seeing the closeness between Jeannie's boys made Katie wish Lucas could feel connected to this family. She called Bertha and wrote Lucas after everyone left.

Two weeks later, Katie woke very nauseated. Jeremy offered a wet washcloth. "You must have the stomach virus that is going around."

She made no reply until the heaves subsided. After rinsing her mouth out, she turned to watch his reaction. "No, this is something I picked up at *the Love Nest*."

Watching as the reality hit was pure delight.

"*Love Nest* baby number two?"

"Close enough."

He hugged her carefully knowing her propensity to upchuck easily. "So when JD and I decide we are interested in a number four, all I have to do is make reservations for *the Love Nest*."

"Let's not share that information, okay?"

He was rubbing her tummy. Webster number three, huh?"

"I wanted to save the surprise for Christmas. Early Merry Christmas, Jeremy."

The nausea continued. Between the baby in her womb and the inquisitive twenty-eight-month-old Jaclyn, Katie had her hands full.

"So what's with the signs on the bathroom doors?" Jeremy asked one evening.

"Jaclyn may look like me, but she has your curious genes. She investigates everything … especially forbidden places and things. Today that included the toilets. Could be we have a future marine biologist.

"I've had to disinfect her and them twice. So all bathroom doors must stay closed. I've had unkind thoughts about parents who use those high latches to secure doors or use indoor play yards to contain their children. I repented today and called to see who carries them. You need to pick up latches after work tomorrow.

"And don't turn your back on her when you take her outside. She's quite fond of Ziggy's food and water, or else she's just a social eater. I could have sworn that her rear was wagging at one point."

Jeremy flipped her braid to the back. "Maybe number three will be the quiet type."

"Possibly. We don't have one of those yet."

The Webster family stayed busy the rest of the winter months and well into spring. The first of May they began preparing the efficiency for Lucas. Two years behind bars had changed the man. Two inmates in his unit had been sharing their faith … and some interesting books.

Jeremy was the one who suggested they haul out the boxes of yellow ribbons and decorate the trees for Lucas. JD's eyes lit up. "He's like the man in the song!"

Katie and Bea made plans to pick him up, May 15, 1999. "Look!

There he is." Their first family meeting outside prison walls was emotional. After wiping tears and sharing individual and group hugs, they made their way to Katie's car. She handed him the keys. "I have your license. Any place you want to go before we head home?"

"Yeah. I'm hungry for a Buster burger."

Bea laughed. "She got me hooked on those habit-forming yummies my last visit." After their stop at Buster's, Lucas headed to Wimberley Estates.

"JD is excited about getting to know his white uncle. And Jaclyn is excited because JD is excited," Katie offered as he turned into the driveway.

Too bad they didn't have a camera to capture the impact the yellow forest had on Lucas. Bea and Katie waited quietly as he drank in the scene. As he faced them tears began forming. "I've been in two kinds of prison in my life. One had walls and bars. The other one held me captive all my life without my knowledge. Today I'm free from both."

Mom, daughter and son spent considerable time tracing God's hand in their lives. Bea offered a prayer of thanksgiving for the freedom from earthly prisons and prisons of the soul.

Bea helped Lucas get settled in the apartment, and then took him to the patio. "Have someone you need to meet." When Ziggy approached, she stepped between her son and the dog. "You and he need to become friends."

"Yeah, I wouldn't want to be his enemy."

While Lucas and Ziggy were getting acquainted, Doc and Jeannie arrived with the younger Websters. JD and Jaclyn stormed the place and spent the rest of the afternoon loving on the newest family member. By the time Jeremy got off work, Lucas was relaxed and enjoying his colorful family.

Racism had been a major problem inside prison. That plus dealing with his dad's hand–me–down bigotry played a big part in opening his eyes to the heart of the problem. The hearts of people. He had to employ Katie's blindfold theory more than once.

As everyone gathered around a rather large dining room table, he glanced at his white sister and mother. "We are outnumbered here, you know?"

Katie reached for his hand. "Lucas, I keep telling you that it's not the color of the skin, but the condition of the hearts. I've found more love in this black family than I ever experienced in my white one and if you'll give them a chance ... so will you."

He scanned the table scene. "For the first time in my life, I feel like I belong. Thank all of you for that."

"I like having a white nana and uncle," JD offered.

"Would that everyone saw each other with the eyes and heart of a child," Doc said as he patted his grandson.

Lucas sat in amazement most of the evening as he watched the ebb and flow of different relationships playing out. He silently thanked God that he was assigned to this family for a year.

After the older Websters went home, he and Bea ended up on the back porch. "I know the weeks and months ahead may not be easy, Mom, but for the first time in my life, I know who I am and who I'm not. A couple of inmates in my unit helped me understand that the missing part of my life has been God. My earthly dad rejected me, but I've met the Father who has always loved me."

Bea didn't try to hide her tears. "I thank God for putting you in the unit with Chad and Justin."

Jeremy joined them. When he heard Lucas' story, he laughed. "You're stuck with me forever now."

Bea was up early the next morning and left for Roanoke when Jeremy departed for work. Lucas, Katie and the children watched and waved. "Come on, Bro. We need to feed your hungry niece and nephew."

Lucas spent the rest of the morning moving the remainder of his belongings into the efficiency. By noon, he had changed into a dress shirt and tie. "I'm on my way to talk with the new bank president, Katie. Hopefully he'll hear me out and give me a chance."

Katie grabbed his hand and prayed. When she finished, he had tears in his eyes. "Thanks, Sis."

It didn't take long for the family and Lucas to adjust to sharing life. As he worked to rebuild his career and livelihood, he also worked hard to be a helpful member of his new family.

As they neared the end of July, Katie's discomfort index was through the roof. She was sitting on the steps on the pool trying to cool off when Jeremy joined her. "How much longer, Babe?"

Katie covered his hand with hers. "It's close, Jeremy. Close."

In the wee hours of the morning, a couple of hard pains roused Katie out of a restless sleep. "Jeremy, wake up." She was shaking her sleeping husband. "The baby. It's time. These pains are hard and coming faster than usual."

The man moved faster than Clark Kent in a phone booth.

"Whoa! We aren't in panic mode here. Call your folks and let Lucas know while I change clothes."

In thirty minutes, Jeremy and Katie were ready to leave. Lucas was in worse shape than Jeremy. "Are you sure we don't need to call an ambulance?" he asked.

Katie waited until the pain subsided. "For you or me, Lucas?" she asked with a smirk.

"For sure one of us will need it if you don't get out of here soon." He grabbed her bag while Jeremy helped her to the car. "I'll call Mom and let her know. Don't worry about the home front. I've got your back." He looked at Jeremy. "Yours too, Brother."

Twenty-Eight

Baby Joshua was born four hours later. All nine pounds and five ounces of him. "I'm voting for girl babies from here on out, Jeremy Webster."

"Honey, after what I watched you endure, I think it's time to let someone else populate the world."

She smiled. "At this moment I agree, but I'm not ready to call it quits yet."

Two days later, Katie and Joshua joined the family at home. The circus wouldn't have produced as much excitement as a new baby did. Both children were hyper. Lucas was quiet. Jeremy supervised *holding time*. When it was Uncle Lucas' time, he put up his hands. "I'm not comfortable holding something that delicate."

Katie's eyes enlarged. "Have you never held a baby?"

"Never."

"Then it's time you did." Katie showed him out to cradle the baby and hold him close. His facial expressions were as comical as his awkward hand and arm movements. "You'll be a pro in no time."

They left Joshua with his uncle until he became restless. "Give him to Mama. He's hungry," JD announced.

Katie and Joshua headed for the bedroom rocker. Jaclyn traipsed behind them. As Katie settled and adjusted Joshua to a breast, her daughter tried to crawl in her lap. "What's he doing, Mama?"

"He's eating, Sweetheart."

Little eyes widened. "Eating you?"

Katie chuckled. "No, there's milk inside mommy's breast."

Her daughter lifted her shirt and looked at her chest. "Do I have milk?"

Katie used her free arm to scoot the female investigator off her lap. "Sweetheart, would you go get Daddy for me?"

Jaclyn ran out of the room. "Daddy, baby eat Mama."

Lucas looked at Jeremy. "She's your daughter."

Jeremy picked up his curious offspring. "Well, you used to eat Mama and look what a fine girl you turned out to be."

Lucas smiled. "That was smart."

"It's the best I can do on such short notice."

Jaclyn's curiosity continued throughout the day. At one point Jeremy turned to Katie. "I'll make you a deal. I'll teach the boys about the birds and the bees if you'll take care of this one's education."

Katie shook her head. "I think we need three more boys to make it even."

Jeremy laughed as he lifted the pint-sized researcher into his arms. "I think she's right, Pumpkin."

Jaclyn put her arms around Jeremy and smiled. "Thank you, Daddy."

Later that night when the children were asleep, Jeremy quizzed Katie. "Will you be able to handle all three during the day?"

"We'll be fine. Lucas will be in and out for a few days, JD is a great little helper and Jaclyn wants to be. I can always call Jeannie if I get desperate."

"Katie, right now I feel like the most blessed man on earth." He stood over Joshua's miniature crib. "He'll grow out of this nest soon."

"That means we'd better get busy moving your workout equipment upstairs so we can get his room ready."

Within three weeks, everyone had adjusted to a new baby in the house and life was back to normal. Granted ... it was a busier normal.

The children were asleep and the adults were enjoying the last hours of the day together. Katie and Jeremy were folding and sorting two baskets of clean clothes.

Lucas was sharing about his job review. "Things are looking up at work. Mr. Johnson said as long as I behave, my future has promise. How are things going for you, Jeremy?"

"I've signed up for a couple of classes at VT this fall. I'm determined to get my law degree within the next few years. Jim and Michael want me to join their firm when I graduate."

"Speaking of lawyers, Dad's trial is coming up in less than two weeks. It looks like they've exhausted all attempts to postpone it again." He sipped his tea and studied his brother. "I can't believe you don't hate the man since hearing Harvey Perkins' confession. Can you believe Dad paid to have you killed?"

"I admit that shook me up some, Lucas, and on more than one occasion I've had to reject hatred where Herbert is concerned. I've witnessed and experienced the poison of hatred and I want no part of it. I hope the jury throws the book at him, but I also pray he repents and seeks forgiveness. Otherwise, his eternity is bleak."

Lucas chewed on those thoughts before continuing. "Did I tell you I met with Rose last week? She had no idea Dad and Edgar raped Jeannie, but she did know Katie and I shared the same mother."

"Rose has not had an easy life, Lucas. Maybe you can share your God story with her," Katie said.

A contemplative expression took over his face. "Now that the shock of our connections has settled and the pieces are coming together, I realize you two and Bea are the only family I have in the world. How crazy is that?"

He glanced toward the bedroom area. "And those kids of yours? I've never loved anyone like I love them. Reckon that's because I'm double kin?" He laughed. "Maybe they should call me Uncle-Uncle Lucas."

"Well, that's good, Bro, because we are getting ready to make out our wills and were wondering if you would be willing to share guardianship with Jeannie and Doc if anything should happen to us."

Moisture gathered in Lucas' green eyes. "You … trust me with your children?"

"Unless you marry someone who is opposed to the idea of beautiful brown children, yes."

"Well, that will have to be one of the stipulations before I get serious then, won't it? God forbid that anything should happen to both of you, but I'd do everything I could."

Lucas looked outside as Ziggy made his presence known. "Does that also include the family pet?"

"Absolutely." Jeremy went to the porch to see what had the dog's attention. Lucas followed. Ziggy ran between the two and back to a spot on the east side of the lawn. He wanted a piece of something.

As Jeremy surveyed the area of Ziggy's interest, he saw movement and a reflection in the woods. He dove for Lucas as the sound of a gunshot filled the night. Lucas went limp. Jeremy grabbed him under the shoulders and dragged him back in the house. "Throw me some towels, Katie, and call 911."

When Katie hung up, she knelt beside Lucas. "Is he going to be okay?"

"Yeah. It creased the side of his head, but somebody wanted him dead."

"Do you think he's still out there?"

"Yes. Listen to Ziggy." They worked with Lucas until a second shot sounded. The dog whimpered before going silent.

"Ziggy!" Katie cried.

Jeremy ran to their bedroom and grabbed his pistol. By the time he opened the front door, a patrol car and ambulance pulled in the driveway. Putting his hand up to shield his eyes from the headlights, he motioned the medics towards the front door. A third shot rang out and Jeremy Webster fell to the ground. A fourth one echoed through the neighborhood, but Jeremy never heard it.

Officer Green pointed the medics to Jeremy while he ran to the edge of the woods. "This one is dead," he reported.

Inside Lucas was coming around but Katie was fighting for control. Her two oldest children were staring at Lucas' bloody head.

"What's going on, Mama?" JD asked.

"Son, take your sister to our bedroom and stay with Joshua until I get there, please."

"Where's Daddy? What's wrong with Uncle Lucas?"

"Remember daddy's talks about emergencies? Obey first and we'll talk later. Please go now. Mama will come tell you as soon as she can."

The troubled boy reached for his sister's hand and disappeared down the hall.

A medic rushed in. "Mrs. Webster, you are needed outside. I'll take care of Lucas."

Katie sprinted out the door as the medics were lifting Jeremy into the ambulance. "Is he alive?" She was touching his bare feet.

"Yes. The bullet struck his leg. He must have hit his head when he fell. We need to get him to the hospital, Ma'am."

Katie stuck her head in the ambulance. "Jeremy Webster, we have come too far for you to quit on me now. You fight this thing."

"Are you coming?" the medic asked.

"I'll have to make arrangements for my children. I'll get there as soon as I can." She jumped out of the way and watched as the ambulance turned on its sirens and lights and disappeared into the night.

Chief Randolph put his arm around her shoulders and pointed her towards her house. "Katie, I called Jeremy's folks. Anyone else I should call?"

She shook her head and fell into his arms. As they walked back towards the house, Katie noticed a body and officers at the edge of the east woods. "Is he dead?"

"Yes, Ma'am."

Katie shuttered and hugged herself. "Do you know him?"

Chief tightened his hold. "Afraid so, Katie. It's Herbert Taylor."

Katie fell to her knees and gave utterance to the anguish this man had inflicted on the people she loved. Her groans silenced the creatures of the night. Suddenly she stilled. "Ziggy!" she shouted. Racing to the side fence, she cried, "Someone check Ziggy."

The chief immediately dispatched a deputy to the backyard. "He's alive," the voice soon replied. Another deputy rushed to help.

As they wrapped the dog in a blanket and put him in the car, Katie lost control. The sound of her pain roused Lucas. "What is going on? Where is Katie?" They could not hold him down, so they helped him to the front door. "What's going on out here?"

Katie ran into his arms. "Thank God, you're okay!"

He moved her to arms' length. "Katie, what happened?"

She couldn't tell him. Chief Randolph pointed to Herbert Taylor's body. "There's not an easy way to say this, Lucas. That is your father."

Lucas pushed away from Katie as understanding dawned. "My dad tried to kill me?" A wild look manifest as he began searching the scene. "Where is Jeremy?"

Tears blurred Katie's vision. "On his way … to the hospital."

"No!" Lucas screamed as he rapidly shook his head from side to side. "Not my dad!" He clutched the front of his shirt as though he was struggling to breathe. He edged closer to the dead body and fell on his knees. With his head resting on Herbert's lifeless body. he sobbed. "Why so much hate, Dad? Why?"

Katie knelt beside him and for the first time since her own daddy's death, wept bitter tears of regret for the wasted lives of both their fathers. With angry eyes, Lucas questioned his sister. "How could God let this happen?"

"Hate, not God, did this, Lucas. And we are not going to cave in to its cruelty. You have a brother and I have a husband who needs us to believe and fight for him right now."

She watched as he slowly made the shift and rose to his feet. "You're right, Sis. Tell me what I need to do."

At that moment, the older Websters exited their vehicle. A weeping Jeannie ran to Katie. "Where are the children?"

All eyes turned towards the house where wide-eyed JD with his teddy bear and sleepy-eyed Jaclyn with her binkie were taking in the scene. "Oh, God, what have they seen?" Katie uttered.

The adults converged on the little ones. Lucas reached for JD as Doc rescued Jaclyn. Jeannie patted Katie's arm. "I will stay with the children. You feed Joshua and go on."

Katie heard Doc as she hurried to Joshua. "Come on, JD. It's too early to be out of bed."

"Where is my daddy, Papa?"

"He got an ouchy and the doctors are making it all better, Son."

"He sure gets lots of ouchys, Papa."

Twenty-Nine

Lucas helped the Websters get the children back to bed, called Bertha and then headed to the hospital. A tearful Jeannie reached for Joshua when he finished eating.

"I'll be back for his next feeding. Lucas said Bea is heading out early tomorrow morning. She'll be a big help."

Jeremy was still in surgery when Katie arrived. "Any word on his injuries?" she asked Doc and Lucas.

"Yeah, he took a bullet to his thigh and sustained a concussion when his head connected with the sidewalk," Doc answered.

As they waited and talked, Katie realized Lucas was fluctuating between hatred for his dad and concern for his brother. "Lucas, this is when we have to submerge ourselves so deeply in God's love that hatred and bitterness can't reach us. Be sad for your dad, but don't partake of his hate. Let that die with him."

The battle was evident in his eyes. "What kind of human tries to kill his own sons?"

Doc put his dark hand on Lucas' white arm. "One who allowed hatred instead of love to fill his heart and mind to the point that evil took over both, Son."

Lucas considered the man who had loved Herbert Taylor's other son as his own flesh and blood. "Got any room in that big heart of yours for another son, Doc?"

A strong, but gentle arm moved to the back of Lucas' shoulders. "Well now, I got myself a mighty fine white daughter. Reckon her brother would make a first-rate number four son."

Lucas studied the dark-skinned man. "What would you say if I changed my last name to Webster?"

Doc's eyes lit up his ebony face. "I'd be honored, Son. Honored."

Katie tried to corral the escaping tears as she answered the ringing phone. "Katie Webster."

"Mrs. Webster, Jeremy is out of surgery. They are now doing a cat scan of his brain to determine the severity of his concussion. You should be hearing from the doctor shortly."

"Thank you."

Within an hour the surgeon walked into the waiting room. "The bullet caused a femoral shaft fracture. I added some hardware to that bone. Recovery will take four to six months. Barring any unexpected complications, his leg should be okay. He might be left with a limp, but it could have been worse. A cat scan of his brain revealed a mild concussion. He should be coming around soon."

Katie offered her hand as tears of gratitude broke loose. "Thank you."

When the doctor left, they shared hugs and shed tears of relief.

"Doc, would you mind calling Jeannie and telling her I'm on my home?"

By the time Katie returned to the hospital after feeding Joshua, Jeremy was waking and calling for her. The nurse ushered her into his cube. Tears of relief trailed down her cheeks as she reached for his limp hand. "Mr. Webster, we have to quit meeting like this."

His eyelids slowly opened and a faint smile emerged. "Hi."

She kissed his lips. "You know you should consider modeling these hospital gowns."

"Funny."

Katie went to the side with less equipment attached. "My

instructions are to see that you rest. So why don't you close those drooping eyelids again and snooze?"

He squeezed her hand. "How's Lucas?"

"With his looks, that snazzy headband may start a new fashion craze. He's fine, Jeremy."

"Katie … ?" His voice trailed off as sleep claimed him again.

She kissed him and joined the men in the waiting area. "Go home, Sis. Joshua needs you. Doc and I are going to take time-about staying here. That frees you to come and go as you can without worry or guilt." He paused and smiled at the dark man at his side. "We'll be here as long as you and Jeremy need us."

Katie's heart warmed. "If you're not careful, I'm going to start liking you."

He stepped out of her reach. "Don't get mushy on me, Sis."

"He doesn't know who did it yet. Think you can handle it if that comes up on your watch?"

Lucas hesitated as he scuffed his shoe on the tile floor. "He saved my life, Katie. We'll deal with Dad together."

Hugging both men before leaving, Katie Webster walked out of Mission Hospital with more joy than sadness and more hope than despair. Love was triumphant. Herbert's seed of hate had no offspring.

Thirty

Bea arrived the morning after the shooting and settled in her favorite upstairs bedroom. By the time Lucas brought Jeremy home a week later, the welcoming group had increased again. James had shown up the day before with a duffle bag as big as he was tall. After announcing he was Jeremy's in-house physical therapist the next four weeks, he bounded up the stairs with an excited nephew and rambunctious niece scrambling behind him. The man was a child magnet.

The entire family was on hand to welcome the last missing family member. Two days after Jeremy's arrival, Officers Lincoln and Abbott delivered a limping, but happy dog. It was difficult to tell who was more thrilled ... the dog ... or his family.

Between James and Lucas helping with Jeremy and Bertha and Jeannie helping around the house, the Jeremy Webster family was doing well. JD was back in school. Jaclyn was thrilled to have more people to entertain. Joshua's immobility and sleeping habits enabled Jeremy to help keep an eye on him.

"This child is going to experience separation anxiety when you have to go back to work," Katie said as she changed the boy's diaper one morning.

When Jeremy didn't respond, Katie turned in his direction. "Don't be upset about needing the workout room to stay downstairs for a few months. Joshua will be fine in here with us."

"I'm okay with that. I like having him close."

"Then what's on your mind?"

"Several things." Katie placed Joshua in the middle of their bed. "One is my concern for Lucas. We've had several talks about Herbert. He still questions God."

As they talked, their attention was drawn to their son. "I can't believe how fast he's growing," Jeremy offered.

"Give Lucas time, Jeremy. He's like this son of yours. He'll grow as he continues to feed on the milk of God's Word, and soon he'll be mature enough to digest the meatier truths."

"Speaking of meatier truths …" He opened the Bible and turned to the section with his yellow ribbon marker. "Listen to this passage in Romans 5. *When we were utterly helpless, Christ came at just the right time and died for us sinners. Now most people would not be willing to die for an upright person, though someone might perhaps be willing to die for someone especially good.*" Jeremy paused and looked at Joshua. "I wouldn't bat an eye to die for our children … or you … or any of my family."

Katie wiped a tear. "Jeremy, as a member of law enforcement, you risk your life every day to protect everyone … not just your family … but also those who hate you. You belong to an elite group of folks as far as I'm concerned."

He fingered the yellow marker. "Sometimes, Katie, I look at you and these children and think how close we came to missing all of this and then how many times we've faced losing it."

"But it's worth it, Jeremy."

"Yeah." He turned back to his Bible. "Listen to the rest of this passage. *For since our friendship with God was restored by the death of His Son while we were still His enemies, we will certainly be saved through the life of His Son.*"

He picked up his notepad and pen and began to draw an illustration of a large ravine between two hills. He wrote the word *man* on one hill and *God* on the other. "That passage says to me that

God used the cross and death of His Son to bridge the gulf between us and Him." He inserted a cross between the two hills and wrote *Jesus* on the horizontal board.

"Because of His great love for us, Jesus laid down his life to become our way back to God and as wonderful as that is, some people still choose darkness. Take Herbert for instance." He closed his Bible.

"Been questioning the Lord about all the troubles that man's hatred brought our way." He closed his eyes and quoted from the first chapter of James, verse two. *When troubles come your way, consider it an opportunity for great joy."*

An amusing smile lit up his face as his clear green eyes danced. "Can you believe that's the verse that came to mind in the midst of my God interrogation?"

Katie chuckled. "Yeah, I rarely find His answers line up with my way of thinking."

"Accepting troubles is one thing, but asking us to do so with joy? That seemed a little farfetched, so I proceeded to remind the Lord of my history with Mr. Taylor. He flooded my mind with all those passages on forgiving and loving my enemies. Forgiving Herbert hasn't been easy, but loving him? I couldn't."

He pulled the yellow ribbon out of the Bible as moisture filled his eyes. "Tell me, Katie, what kind of love drives a person to lay down his life for people who will never change? Jesus embodied that kind of love. His cross was covered with ribbons of forgiveness and love for every prisoner of sin, including Herbert.

"Two days of wrestling and God and I agreed on one thing. I had a love and vision problem. Not only did I not love Herbert with God's love, I wasn't viewing my life through God's eyes.

"I spent the next day in God's operating room where He used Isaiah 45:3 to cut away the cataracts of religion and human reasoning that have kept me blind to the treasures He gave me in my dark seasons. *And I will give you treasures hidden in the darkness … secret riches. I will do this so you may know that I am the Lord."*

He wiped a tear. "It's amazing how looking back with a different heart and vision changes everything. My feelings of always being someone's target gave way to counting it great joy. That's hindsight. God through the writings of James asks us to have foresight. Count it joy before the earthly reality is evident."

Katie's eyes filled with tears. "That's what the writer of Hebrews was trying to tell us. *Because of the joy awaiting him, Jesus endured the cross.* Jesus saw beyond his death, beyond the grave." A tear broke free. "Jeremy … He … saw … us."

Jeremy handed her a tissue. "I'm glad he said *endure.* He didn't minimize the pain caused by the dark times."

Katie wiped the tears trickling down his cheeks. "Jeremy, our parentage, all of our hard times, all of our fearful moments, learning to forgive our enemies, and even love them, all of our still unanswered questions … everything makes sense."

Jeremy was watching Joshua. "Yes, and God willing, we are going to learn to count it joy in the middle of future dark seasons." He carefully placed the yellow ribbon back in his Bible. "At first the ribbons represented yours and God's forgiveness and love. After this week, they also remind me that God's light shines brightest in our dark seasons."

Katie retrieved a cd and slipped it into the player. Soon the words of the Judds' popular song began to fill the room. *Love Can Build A Bridge.* "The writers of that song got it right, Jeremy. *Only love can join the tribes of man.*"

They listened and hummed along as the song took on new significance. "Ever notice the spiritual overtones of some secular music?" Katie asked.

"Not until now." Joshua was stirring again. "Is it feeding time?" Jeremy asked.

"Close to it."

When Katie and Joshua settled in their eating chair … as Jaclyn called it … Jeremy grabbed his notepad and began making notes.

The days passed and Jeremy continued to improve. The children loved having Daddy home. Having Uncle James and Nana Bea were added bonuses.

Jeremy had been home five weeks. James had decided to hang around a few more weeks to help with his therapy.

Katie and Bertha were cleaning the aftermath of breakfast. Lucas had taken JD to school. James had gone to get Jeremy ready for their first therapy session of the day. Jaclyn was in her booster chair still eating and entertaining nine-week-old Joshua who was in his bouncy chair atop the table.

The door chimes sounded. "Who could that be?" Katie asked as she grabbed a towel to dry her hands.

"I'll get it, Katie," she heard James say.

The women listened as soft voices chatted at the doorway. "Watch the children. I'm going to check out the early birds."

Bea smiled. "Good. I'm curious too."

When Katie made the turn from the eating area of the house into the large foyer, she saw Jeannie, Doc and James huddled together. Were they crying?

"What's going on?" she asked.

A sober Doc stepped forward. "Come with me, Katie."

She fell in step as he walked into the sleeping area of the downstairs. James moved to her other side as they neared the master suite. Both men stepped back as she entered. Jeremy was in the floor at the foot of the bed. Katie rushed to his side. "Jeremy, what happened?" As she touched his body, she felt the breath leave hers. "Oh, God! Why now?"

She reached for his limp hand ... kissed his lifeless lips ... and fell apart. When she regained her composure, James knelt beside her.

"What happened? Were you here?" she asked.

He helped her up. "He was gone when I got here. Probably a blood clot, Katie. I called Mom and Dad before telling you. I hope you're not upset with me. I wanted them here when you found out. The ambulance will be here soon, but I won't let them in until you're ready."

She knew James was trying to be strong for her. She reached for his hands. "It's okay, James. I'm grateful you are here and taking charge. Thank you."

He pulled her into his arms, and they shared the pain of losing a husband and a brother.

Jeannie stood over her son before turning to Katie. "In spite of the way he was conceived, Jeremy was God's gift to all of us." She waited until Katie's eyes met hers. "And look at what he gave us. You and three beautiful children."

Their last serious conversation began echoing inside Katie's head. "He was the treasure hidden in the darkest night of your life, Jeannie."

Jeannie was wiping her tears and Katie's with the same handkerchief. "Yes, Child, he was and now you and these children are our treasures in this dark hour."

Katie collapsed in Jeannie's arms. "What would I do without you and Doc?"

Jeannie thanked God for Jeremy and the family he left behind and then she prayed for all of them.

"Jeannie, not only were you part of Jeremy's earthly treasures, you and your family are a big part of mine. I'm blessed to be a Webster."

After the other three had said their goodbyes, they left Katie alone. She dropped into Jeremy's chair and reached for his Bible. As she flipped through the pages, a sheet of folded paper slipped out. There was writing on the front and the back. It was titled, *Treasures in My Darkness.*

Tears rolled as she traced each name and event listed. Pressing the sheet of paper to her chest, she prayed. *Help me find the treasures in this scary darkness, Lord.*

Katie stooped beside his body. "I can't bring myself to say goodbye, Jeremy." She ran her fingers through his hair and traced every feature of his face. "Thanks for loving me when the world shouted *no*. Our children will always remind me of you and us. Raising them without you scares me."

She stopped to blow her nose and wipe her tears. "Only death could have separated us, but even that can't stop the crazy, wonderful love we shared. I will always love you."

She kissed him one last time before walking into the foyer. James rose to meet her. "The ambulance is outside, Katie."

"Tell them Turner Funeral Home will be in charge when they finish the autopsy. And James, tell Isaac I want Jeremy's coffin covered with a massive spray of yellow roses and ribbon."

"What about JD and Lucas, Katie?" James asked.

"Let's wait until they get home."

James picked up JD after school. The kid's face lit up when he saw the family gathered. "Hi, everybody! Is it chicken and dumpling night?"

Struggling to restrain her tears, Katie patted the seat next to her. "How about a hug? And then we need to talk."

Little brown arms wrapped around her neck, but his eyes were searching the room. "Is Daddy sleeping?"

Katie pulled her eight-year-old son into her lap. "It's Daddy we need to talk about, JD." She took a deep breath and prayed for courage and the right words. "You know how much we love Daddy?"

"Yeah, bunches."

In spite of her resolve tears escaped.

"Mama, has something happened to my daddy again?"

"Daddy is with Jesus, JD."

Big tears formed in his eyes. "Does that mean he's dead, Mama?"

"That's what we call it here, JD, but your daddy is more alive than he's ever been."

Between sniffs and sobs, the little boy asked. "Is that why he's been talking to me about heaven?"

Katie stammered. "Y-y-your daddy … has been talking to you … about heaven?"

JD was trying to be brave. "Yeah, ever since the bad man shot him and Uncle Lucas, he's been telling me what a neat place it is."

Katie wrapped her arms around JD and smiled through her tears. "Well, he's taking his first tour about now, Honey, and I suspect he's wishing we were with him."

"He's not coming back, is he?"

"No, Son. Someday we will join him."

"Then bad people can't ever hurt him again, can they, Mama?" Tears were dripping off his brown cheeks.

"That's right, JD. No one can ever hurt your daddy again."

"I'm glad about that part." He wiped his tears and a slight smile broke through his sadness. "And I'm glad we found him before Jesus took him to heaven."

Mother and son hugged and wept for a long time before JD pulled back some. "Is it alright if I cry, Mama? Daddy would want me to be a big boy, but sometimes it's hard."

A teary-eyed James sat beside them and reached for his nephew. "Come on, JD. We'll cry together while we play some basketball. Okay?"

He lunged into James' arms. "Okay, Uncle James. Are you going away too?"

"Not today, Buddy, not today."

Katie took Joshua to their bedroom while Bea, Jeannie and Doc occupied Jaclyn. Had Jeremy sensed his time was near? Or did God use him to prepare her and JD?

Bea and Jeannie had JD's favorite supper going when Lucas stormed through the passage between his place and the main house. "It's official," he said as it waved a piece of paper in the air. "I'm now a Webster."

The announcement he thought would bring cheers caused an eruption of tears. He surveyed the room. "Where is Jeremy?"

JD jumped out of Doc's lap and rushed to his Uncle. "He's with Jesus." And the tear flow started again.

Lucas swept the weeping nephew in his arms. "With Jesus?"

"Yeah, he's gone." Small arms circled Lucas neck. "You're not going to live with Jesus today, are you, Uncle Lucas?"

Wild, angry eyes landed on Katie. "God wouldn't want me right now, JD. I'm not real happy with His decision."

A waterlogged Katie leaped to her feet and moved close to Lucas and JD. Doc followed. With trembling hands on his arm she pleaded, "Remember all those talks you and he had? Don't let hate gain a foothold today."

Doc stepped on the other side. "Death tries to make us feel like evil won, Son, but love is not only stronger than hatred, it's stronger than the grave. Love never dies, Lucas. It multiples in the soil of God's love and reproduces many seeds. You, Lucas Webster are proof that love is stronger than hate. Now you can prove it's stronger than the grave. Don't let your brother's life and death be in vain."

The white man with eyes so like Jeremy's and JD's, melted in the black arms of Jeremy's father ... and now his.

Thirty-One

With the love and help of family and friends and the God of all comfort, Katie, the children and Jeremy's family learned to live without him. Against Katie's protest, James resigned his position in California and found employment in the Asheville area. He bought a condominium mid-way between his job site and Katie's place. He was now as much a part of their lives as Lucas was. "I promised Jeremy I'd help you raise these children if anything ever happened to him, Katie, and I intend to keep that promise ... with or without your approval."

She searched the eyes of the man who was present the night Jeremy was conceived. "When did you have that conversation?"

"Came up during one of his therapy sessions." He studied her a few seconds. "Katie, I think all smart police officers have conversations like that. Look at Mark's family."

"I know, but sometimes I wonder if Jeremy sensed his time was near."

James stared at nothing in particular for a few seconds. "I don't think so. He was too happy to have had those kinds of feelings and thoughts. I think he was just being realistic."

Katie and Lucas talked Bertha into selling her place in Roanoke and moving upstairs. James and Doc did some remodeling and turned two of the bedrooms with a bath into a lovely suite. That left Katie and the children in the four bedrooms downstairs. All shared the general living area.

The days turned into weeks and the weeks became months. Somehow, they made it through the first year. JD didn't cry as much now. His uncles and Papa were never far away. Jaclyn had asked about her daddy when it first happened, but it wasn't long before her questions ceased. Joshua would never know the beautiful man who proudly called him *Son*.

On the first anniversary of Jeremy's home going, Katie retrieved the boxes of yellow ribbons from the attic. "What if we decorate the trees today to celebrate your daddy's earthly life and his first year with Jesus?" Everyone agreed.

That evening they watched some family videos and perused some photo albums. Four-year-old Jaclyn pointed to Jeremy and smiled. "Daddy."

When the children insisted the ribbons had to go up the second year, Katie didn't object. Keeping Jeremy's memory alive was important.

With his probation ending in May, Lucas bought a condominium next to James. Bea moved into the efficiency. Once again, the upstairs became living quarters for Webster family reunions. Jeannie and Doc remained an integral part of the family.

The second year passed with fewer tears and more acceptance. That was the year Jeannie and Bea convinced Katie she needed a life outside her children. A part-time job with a local design group proved to be what the doctor ordered.

Today was the third anniversary of Jeremy's death. At JD's insistence, the yellow ribbons were donning the trees again. Nana Bea was supervising swim time. Katie was putting the finishing touches on supper when the doorbell rang. Lucas or James was probably hungry for a home cooked meal. Those men needed to find a good wife.

Katie opened the door and her mouth at the same time. "Lucas ..." Hands covered her mouth as the shock of seeing Kyle hit. "What are you doing here?"

Her spontaneous greeting embarrassed both of them. "When I told Aunt Bea I was going to be in the area on business the next few days, she suggested I drop in. I'm sorry, Katie. I should have called you first. From the looks of your lawn you folks are celebrating something."

Ashamed of her rudeness, she stepped aside and motioned for him to enter. "No, no. Don't mind me. I figured it was Lucas or James. Come on in. Bea is out back with the children. Do you remember the way?" She pointed to the double doors at the back of the house.

"Yeah, thanks." He didn't linger.

Business in the area? Was his wife with him? Katie watched from a distance as Kyle stood on the porch. When JD spotted him, he leaped out of the pool and rushed to open arms. "Kyle!"

He moved the wet youngster to arms' length. "I can't believe how big you are. How old are you now?"

"Eleven." JD stayed close as six-year-old Jaclyn joined them. "Who are you?"

Kyle knelt and reached for the dark-skinned replica of Katie. "My name is Kyle. What's yours?"

"Jaclyn, but you can call me Jackie."

"Do you give hugs, Jackie?" Kyle asked. Without hesitation, she walked into big, strong arms and did not back away after they shared a hug. Kyle stood with her cradled in his right arm and her arm around his neck.

Bea approached with her three-year-old grandson.

"And who is this fine looking young man?" Kyle asked.

"His name is Joshua, but we call him Josh," JD answered.

When Joshua leaned towards Kyle, the man opened his other arm and nestled the good size child close to his chest. "How are you, Josh?"

Without saying a word, the boy gave him a big hug.

Bea spoke up. "Katie, I invited Kyle to join us for supper, is that okay?"

JD butted in. "Please, Mom."

"Sure. I'll set another place while everyone washes their hands." With that, she exited the scene miffed that Bea had not alerted her ahead of time.

Thankfully, her children jabbered and Bea carried the responsibility for the table conversation. Her thoughts and emotions were in such disarray that she was afraid to open her mouth … to eat or speak. Kyle, on the other hand, ate heartily and interacted with Bea and the children with ease.

Aunt Bea insisted on cleaning up the kitchen and shooed them into the hearth room. The children clung to Kyle like flies caught on sticky paper. He entertained them by constructing intricate buildings and interesting objects out of all their building toys. Katie watched quietly.

"Katie, what if I give Josh and Jackie their baths and get them ready for bed while you and JD visit with Kyle?" Bea asked when she rejoined them.

"No, Kyle is *your* guest. I'll do that." Katie said rather curtly as she picked up Joshua. "Say goodnight, Son."

When Kyle reached out, Josh went limber leaning towards the open arms. Little arms circled his neck.

"Goodnight, Josh." And he planted a quick kiss on his head.

Katie retrieved the limber body. "Bath time, Son."

Jaclyn was snug in Kyle's lap. "Night, Mr. Kyle. Will you come see us again?"

Kyle risked a glance at Katie. "I'm not sure, Honey." He kissed another little head.

Katie and the two younger ones left JD and Bea with Kyle. After they chatted and played some, JD led Kyle into his room to show him pictures of his daddy. "I miss him, Kyle. Mama misses him, too. She still cries sometimes … like today. Jackie and Josh don't even remember him. A bad man killed him. Officer Lincoln killed the bad man."

When big tears began rolling down the kid's cheeks, Kyle pulled him into his arms. "Your daddy loved you and your mama very much, JD. He would be real proud of the fine young man you are today."

"I know, but he's gone. We need a new daddy. Long time ago you wanted to be my daddy. Are you still interested?"

"I don't think your mother is, JD."

"She's not. Uncle James offered to be my daddy. Mama said he would always be her brother and my uncle." A smile that almost brought tears to Kyles' eyes lit up the boy's face. "I prayed you'd come and you did. Now I'm going to pray she changes her mind."

That was the moment Katie stuck her head in the door. "Hey, I hate to break up this man thing you two have going on, but it's getting late and the younger male here needs to take his bath and get to bed."

"Mom, is it okay if Kyle comes for supper tomorrow?"

Katie brushed her hands through his curls. "If that's what you want, JD."

The boy hugged his mom and then Kyle. "Can you?"

"Your mom and I will discuss it, JD."

Disappointment replaced his smile as he faced Katie. "I want him to come, Mom."

JD grabbed his pajamas and headed for the bathroom as Katie and Kyle walked out of the sleeping quarters. "What brings you to Asheville, Kyle?"

"I'm buying out the Sykes and James Design firm in town."

Katie stopped in her tracks. "I work for them."

The big man's deep blue eyes met hers. "I know. I saw a list of their employees. That's why I called Bea. Looks like I'm going to be your boss again. Think you can handle that?"

"Depends. Is this a long distance investment or do you plan on living here?"

"Definitely an investment. I'd like to leave Denver, but not sure where I'll end up."

"How does your wife feel about leaving Denver?"

Kyle's hands were in and out of his pockets a few times before he found the courage to speak. "Katie, my marriage lasted nine months. I have no wife or children."

When they joined Bea in the hearth room, she excused herself for the night. "Katie, I'm taking my weary body to the shower and then finding a good book to read before I hit the sack. Good to see you, Kyle."

"Take care, Aunt Bea," Kyle offered.

Katie and Bea exchanged a look that held promise of a future, heated exchange.

Strained silence filled the air. Scooting forward on his seat and clearing his throat caused Katie to glance towards the uninvited visitor. "We might as well clear the air, Katie. Your suspicions are correct. Bea planned this meeting and insisted I not call you in advance. That was wrong and I apologize."

Katie softened some. "Apology accepted. My children enjoyed your visit."

Kyle rose to his feet and began rubbing the back of his neck. "I'm here for a reason, Katie. I hope by the time my story ends, you'll understand and forgive Aunt Bea."

He stared out the window before turning to face her. "I've gone over this conversation a hundred times in my head, but right now I'm tongue tied."

He moved to the closest chair. "Katie, our last day together seven years ago changed my life forever. Up until that time, I considered myself a relatively good person with better morals than most and far more money and opportunities than anyone deserves. Yet the one thing I wanted above all else … you … I lost. My world fell apart and bitterness became my mistress. I was angry with you and my folks, and I hated Jeremy Webster."

Katie stiffened.

"I made a lot of stupid decisions after that, including marrying Bernice. She was wrong from the beginning and I knew it, but at the time … I didn't care. Nine months later, we were divorced. That was my wake-up call and Aunt Bea became my *Dear Abby*. She challenged me to quit hating long enough to consider the difference between the man you chose and the one you rejected. 'You're smart, Kyle Butler,' she said. 'What did Jeremy Webster offer Katie that all your money and power couldn't? Figure that out and the rest will come easily.'

"What drew you to him became my consuming quest. I subscribed to your local newspapers. I kept up with everything happening in your lives. I hired a private investigator to dig into Jeremy's past. Found out about his impressive football and Marine days. His time with the police force. Even his engagement to Valerie. I left no stone unturned. He had very little of this world to offer. His skin and rank in life didn't matter to you, and my wealth and position didn't impress you.

"And then the unthinkable happened. He died. My attention turned immediately to you. I wanted to rush to your rescue, but even before Bea pointed out that you would reject me again, I knew that was true.

"All those years I had blamed Jeremy for losing you and suddenly it was clear the problem had not been him, but me. Aunt Bea says that's when I began to change."

Katie's waterlogged eyes were now leaking. She blew and wiped the moisture away only to have to wipe again. "What changed, Kyle?"

"Everything, Katie. My heart. My mind. My hopes and dreams. You should have seen me the day it dawned on me that Jeremy Webster was heir to riches that far surpassed all our Butler wealth."

He moved beside her. "That was the day I also had to admit you made the right choice. Not only could you not fill the God hole in me, but your rejection became the catalyst of my personal God search.

"Think about it, Katie. If not for Jeremy, more than likely both of us would have missed knowing God. I've not only forgiven you and Jeremy, I thank God He brought both of you into my life." He stood and shoved his hands in his pockets. "And that's what I came to say."

Katie couldn't hold back the tears nor speak. *Here is another treasure hidden in our darkness, Jeremy.* Kyle waited quietly as she regained her composure.

"Thank you for sharing your story. Maybe someday I'll share

mine, but not tonight. I need to spend some time with JD before he goes to sleep."

Kyle asked rather reluctantly, "Are you okay with my coming for supper tomorrow night?"

Katie responded impulsively. "As long as you and Aunt Bea understand I'm not in the market for a husband."

A gentleness she recalled from years ago radiated from the man. "Katie, I didn't come here shopping for a wife. I came to share how God had used you and Jeremy to turn my life around and to alert you that we would be seeing each other occasionally at work. I'm sorry if I left any other impression."

His kind and honest reply humbled her. "Kyle, that was a rude and arrogant statement. Forgive me."

Eyes filled with compassion met hers. "Already have."

Their walk to the door was quiet. Kyle glanced at the yellow-clad trees. "What's with the ribbons, Katie?"

"JD's way of celebrating his dad's life on the anniversary of his death." She placed a hand on his arm. "Thank you for coming tonight, Kyle. You brought sunshine into a day of bitter-sweet memories."

Kyle stared into the shadows of the night for a few seconds before turning back to face her. "Tell your son I'll see him tomorrow evening."

"We eat at six o'clock."

"Goodnight, *Mrs. Webster,*" he offered with a slight bow and a charming smile before walking away.

"Goodnight, Mr. Butler," Katie whispered as his truck disappeared into the darkness of the night.

"My thoughts are nothing like your thoughts," says the Lord.
And my ways are far beyond anything you could imagine.
For just as the heavens are higher than the earth,
so my ways are higher than your ways
and my thoughts higher than your thoughts.
Isaiah 55:8-9 (NLT)

Dear Reader,

My first introduction to another race happened when I was a small child. In the middle of a splattering of houses in a rural community of East Tennessee sat the home of Doc and Jeannie, a black couple. Our backyard and theirs joined. Doc was the quiet custodian for our local grammar school. He kept us warm and our surroundings clean. Jeannie had two attributes that impacted me for life. She was the happiest person I knew or have known since, and she knew God on a level that no one else around me did.

When I came to a crisis of faith my second of year of college, it was her simple faith and life that pulled me back to a place of choosing to believe and trust God for what I did not yet understand.

It should not have come as a surprise when God opened the doors for us to adopt a baby from Central America back in the 70s. Our daughter is one of the most beautiful persons I know ... inside and out. She dated whites, blacks and Hispanics. It was the latter she married and they have given us a handsome, dark-skinned grandson. I can't imagine life without them.

I'm white. I have not personally experienced the pain of racism even though I have walked with loved ones who have. My dear, white friends, sympathy and compassion do not give us understanding of their reality any more than watching the birth of a baby compares to having one. Understanding and accepting that fact goes a long way in forging relationships.

I know there are many facets to the problem of racism, but I believe the heart of the problem involves the hearts of people. And that will only be remedied one heart at a time.

The Bible assures us Heaven will be filled with a rainbow of colors. Revelation 5:9b *For you were slaughtered, and your blood has ransomed people for God from every tribe and language and people and nation.* Why do we think it should be any different here?

Is it possible God deposits a foretaste of eternity into our relationships when we reach across the wasteland of ignorance and hate to embrace another race in friendship or marriage?

The year spent writing this story was also spent praying it becomes a bridge that unites those God never intended to be divided. In Christ Jesus, we are ONE.

If this story, *Callie's Treasures*, or *Jake and Josie's Discovery* has touched your heart, would you do me a favor? Leave a message at pricejb490@gmail.com or a review on Amazon.com or westbowpress.com.

My books are available in all three formats from Westbow Press and other outlets like Amazon.com. Westbow offers discounts to ministries.

The sequel to this one, *Kyle's Secret*, is on the burner. Until then, God bless.

Acknowledgements

God the Father, Jesus the Son and the Holy Spirt, thank you for being the example of perfect love and inviting all races into your family circle.

Doc and Jeannie, thank you for loving the little, white girl next door and being examples of God's love in her most impressive years. Put me on your heavenly calendar. I want to spend an eon or two catching up.

Jennifer, Christian and Jackson, you add color to our pale-faced family. Our lives are richer and our hearts bigger because of you.

Michael and Linda, you and yours are such a part of our hearts that even death will not separate us, and heaven will witness our reunion.

Terry, Elaine and Tandra, thinking of you always makes me smile … inside and out. We are family and I love you for including me in yours.

Bonnie and Debbie, you were the first racially mixed couple that I knew personally. Always loved it that we share the same last name.

My black MTSU family, Les, Reggie, Rufus and Shirley, Linda, Gladys, Ron, Rita, Dr. Kim, Mary, Kevin, my years there would have been colorless without you. Even now thoughts of you elicit a chuckle.

Thomas, Herman, the Bailey family, the Bonner family, the Lyles family, though it was the work place that brought you into our lives, it was your openness to us that has kept you in our hearts.

Charles and Sharon, the years and miles that have separated us physically have not extracted you from our hearts. After all, you introduced me to my first computer and the Brooklyn Tabernacle Choir.

Lokelani, you've brought a touch of the islands into my life. I love to watch you dance before our Lord.

Dr. Gresham, God has used you to save my life and help me maintain a healthier lifestyle. I respect you as my cardiologist. I cherish you as my friend.

Rachel and family, though white like me, your eyes see the beauty of all of God's people and your heart reaches across the gulf that divides. I'm honored to call you and yours … family.

Linda, Jennifer, Lisa, Pat, and Sarah, only you five know the impact your input had on this book. Thank you for your honesty, your insight, your foresight, your questions, your encouragement. Thank you for investing in it and believing in me.

Jayne, Lisa, Pat and Joyce, my faithful prayer partners, only heaven knows the effect your prayers have on these stories.

Ladies of the 2015 retreat, thank you for participating in the introduction of the third book. You were the reason the first book was written three years ago. Many of your stories were woven into the second one. Some of you have been part of all three. Without question, you are among my most ardent encouragers. Thank you.

Barry, husband of fifty-one years, thank you for sharing all the seasons of life with me. This last one has stretched both of us. I will always love you.

Westbow Press, without you none of this would have happened. Thank you.

About the Author

Writing was never on JB's bucket list. After all, she was a teacher, not a writer. She dismissed every suggestion to the contrary until two days after her seventy-first birthday.

That was the day she gave the storyline in her head permission to exit. *Callie's Treasures* was the result. After months of revisions and several public readings, she entered the world of self-publishing at the urging of those who heard or read the story. The sequel, *Jake and Josie's Discovery*, followed the next year. And now *Katie's Surprise* joins the list.

JB acknowledges her lack of professional training and regrets any migraines her work gives trained writers and editors. As she continues to delve into this unexpected, late-life adventure, she is hopeful the level of her work increases.

Meanwhile, she prays the truths embedded in the stories—the reason she writes—touch hearts by generating hope to the hurting and gratitude to the healed.

JB and her husband of fifty-one years live on a small farm in Rutherford County, Tennessee.